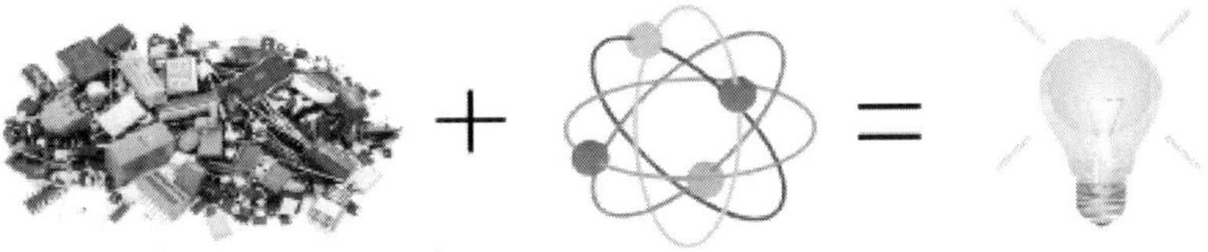

HackingPhysics Journal

Vol.1, no 1

Jan 2020

Simple, Low-Cost and High-Performance Arduino Analog Measurements

Eric Bogatin

www.HackingPhysics.com

978-1-7344059-6-5

The HackingPhysics Journal

A research report from the HackingPhysics Lab

A publication of Addie Rose Press

Addie Rose Press

The HackingPhysics Journal is a periodic publication from the HackingPhysics Lab, published by Addie Rose Press.

Each issue focuses on a specific topic related to the combination of low-cost electronics and physics to empower the reader to dive into more detail exploring the world around us.

Each issue includes all the details about the hardware and software tools, enough of the principles to use them effectively, examples of science experiments anyone can do with these tools and some indications of where experimenters can explore further.

It is meant as the missing manual.

Table of Contents

Chapter 1. **In This Issue**

In this publication, I show you how to use both the built in 10-bit ADC and an external16-bit ADC with an Arduino Uno microcontroller board to master analog measurements.

All the instructions and sketches needed to measure, analyze, print, plot and save your measurements in a data file or directly in excel are included in this eBook.

In each sketch I provide, you can literally copy the sketch from this eBook, paste it into a blank sketch in the Arduino IDE and it will just work.

Here is an example of what is ahead for you in this publication:

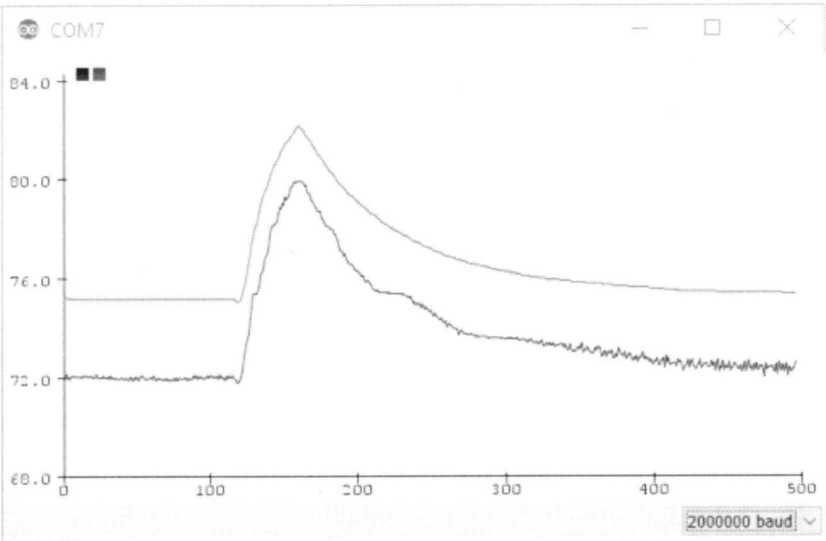

Figure 1.1. Measurements of the same TMP36 sensor at the same time by the 10-bit ADC (blue) and the 16-bit ADC (red).

Analog measurements are at the core of microcontroller applications. Afterall, most systems consist of a sensor, a controller and an actuator, with or without feedback between them.

Many sensors, which translate the physical world into an electrical quality, create an analog voltage signal. The way this gets into the controller's world of digital bits is with an analog to digital converter (ADC).

Built into the Atmega 328 microcontroller is a 10-bit ADC. Using the techniques illustrated in this publication, we'll see how to get the most out of this simple to use feature.

For many applications, 10-bit resolution, or the ability to measure 5 mV increments in voltage, is just fine. For others, higher resolution is a must.

After I illustrate how to get the most out of the 10-bit, built in ADC, I'll introduce you to the simplest to use, lowest cost 16-bit ADC available so you will quickly be taking measurements with a resolution which can be less than 20 uV and noise floor of less than 10 uV rms with averaging.

Using these two ADC devices, I show you in this publication how to:

- ✓ *Instantly measure, print and plot analog measurements with three lines of code*
- ✓ *Increase the sample rate of the built in 10-bit ADC by more than a factor of 7*
- ✓ *Average consecutive readings based on a fixed number of averages*

- ✓ *Average consecutive readings over a time interval defined as an integral number of power line cycles to eliminate 60 Hz pick up*
- ✓ *Calibrate the 10-bit ADC using the 3.3 V power rail on the Arduino board*
- ✓ *Easily process the measurements to change the units based on a conversion factor*
- ✓ *Use a low-cost 16-bit ADC and acquire data 3x faster than the default acquisition speed*
- ✓ *Print the data to the serial monitor*
- ✓ *Plot the data on the serial plotter as a scope or as a strip chart recorder*
- ✓ *Data log the data into a text file*
- ✓ *Print the data directly into excel and plot it in real time and save into an excel file*

Chapter 2. **Quick Start with the Built-in 10-bit ADC**

If you are not familiar with some of the basic operations of the Arduino, check out the first book in the *Saturday Afternoon Low-Cost Electronics Projects* series, Arduinos Without Tears.

The Arduino communicates with the outside world with voltages. Digital voltages are written and read with the digital I/O pins. In addition, we can read analog voltages with the analog to digital converter (ADC).

These voltages can come from a variety of sources. The more interesting ones are from sensors that translate some aspect of the physical world into an electrical signal.

The ADC, which reads analog voltages, built into every Arduino board, is really easy to use. You can get started measuring your first voltages and print or plot your first voltage measurements in about one minute.

In this chapter, we will:

- ✓ *Measure a voltage as a digital level*
- ✓ *Plot it on the serial plotter*
- ✓ *Display the level value and when it was recorded on the serial printer*
- ✓ *Copy this data from the serial monitor and paste it into excel*

✓ *Plot it in excel*

2.1 New hardware feature: the ADC

Built into every Arduino microcontroller is a special section of the chip that will measure the voltage on an input pin. This voltage is called an *analog signal*, as distinct from a digital signal.

Digital signals have only one of two values, a LOW or a HIGH, a logical 0 or a logical 1. In the Arduino Uno board, the voltage of a logical 1 signal is 5 V and the voltage of logical 0 signal is 0 V.

That's it. Those are our only choices in a digital signal.

Analog signals can have almost any value within some range. To be read directly by an Arduino, the voltage level is limited to between 0 V and 5 V, but we can measure many different values between these limits. Figure 2.1 illustrates how the voltage of a digital and analog signal might vary over time.

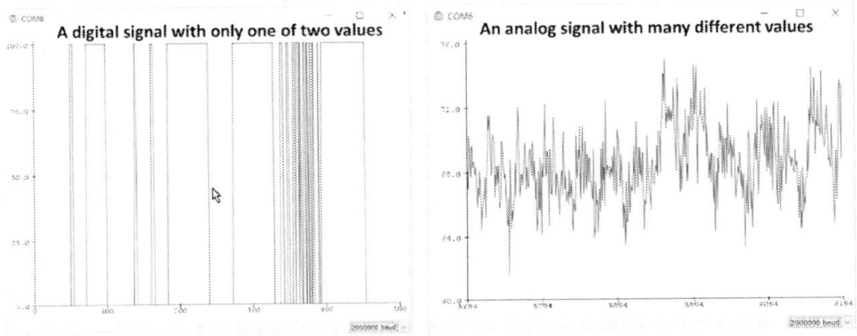

Figure 2.1. An example of a digital signal (left) and an analog signal (right).

The analog voltage is measured and converted into digital information to then be interpreted by the Arduino, with the *analog to digital converter* (ADC) circuit built into the Arduino microcontroller chip.

The ADC in the Arduino Uno is able to measure a voltage with 10-bit resolution. This means the voltage is read and converted into $2^{10} = 1024$ different levels, ranging in value from 0 to 1023.

When we read a voltage value with an ADC, what the Arduino gives back to us is an integer corresponding to the level between 0 and 1023. These values correspond to an input voltage of about 0 to 5 V. This means each level corresponds to a voltage change of 5 V/1023 = 4.89 mV/ADU.

When the ADC measures a voltage on one of the specific analog input pins, labeled as A0 to A5, located in the lower right side of the board shown in Figure 2.2, it is always the difference in voltage between that pin and the ground pin on the Arduino board.

Figure 2.2. The Arduino Uno with the analog pins in the lower right of the board identified by the square.

2.2 Taking your first ADC measurements and display them on the serial monitor

In the Arduino Uno, there is really just one analog to digital converter (ADC) built into the microcontroller. But, there are six different pins to which it can connect.

When we command the Arduino to take an analog reading, we are really telling the ADC to which pin to connect the ADC and then take the reading. On the Atmega 328 microcontroller chip, the brains of the Arduino Uno board, there is one ADC and a switch which connects one of the six analog pins into the ADC, one at a time.

This means we can only take readings from one analog pin at a time. The switch can connect the ADC to a specific analog pin pretty quickly. It can connect and take a reading in about 112 microseconds. This is about 8,900 times a second. We'll see how to measure this sampling rate, and how to speed it up considerably in the next chapter.

In the Arduino board, all six of the analog pins that connect to the ADC are available to sensors. We identify them and select them by their analog pin number, A0, A1,...A5.

To read the voltage on any pin, we use the command,

```
analogRead(pinNumber);
```

The pin labels shown on the side of the pins on the board, are the pin numbers we use in the command to read that pin. This command will return the value read by the ADC as an integer number from 0 to 1023. I call these units analog to digital units, or _ADU.

Every time we call the analogRead() command, we take a reading from the specified ADC pin and store this number in the command. We could just print this value each time we read it.

To take a reading on analog pin A0, and print the value to the serial monitor, is literally one line of code:

```
Serial.println(analogRead(A0));
```

Try this experiment: Write a sketch that sets up the Arduino to print the value on the analog pin A0 and plots it on the serial monitor, as fast as it can.

The whole sketch is only six lines, including all the brackets. Here is my version:

```
void setup() {
  Serial.begin(2000000);
}
void loop() {
  Serial.println(analogRead(A0));
}
```

You can literally copy this sketch from this eBook, paste it in a blank sketch and push the Upload button. It will immediately be uploaded and just run.

Try this experiment. After the sketch is done uploading, open up the serial monitor by selecting under Tools/Serial Monitor.

Make sure the baud rate is set the same in the lower right of the serial monitor as you wrote in the sketch. In my sketch, this is 2000000.

If you have never done this before, you should check out more details in the first book in the *Saturday Afternoon Low-Cost Electronics Projects* series, Arduinos Without Tears.

You should see a string of numbers displayed on the screen. What do you think you are measuring? Here's a hint, 60 Hz pick up.

Congratulations, you've taken your first measurements from the ADC pin and printed out the values.

2.3 Plotting the data on the serial plotter

I prefer to see data plotted, using the serial plotter feature. Looking at a plot makes it so much easier to discern patterns in the data than seeing a bunch of numbers scrolling by.

The serial plotter turns your screen into a strip chart recorder. Don't forget to set the baud rate on the serial plotter screen to 2000000. The voltage appearing on the A0 pin of the Arduino board will be plotted on the strip chart screen and auto scaled.

Also, be aware that if you want to turn on the serial plotter, you have to close the serial monitor first. They can't both be open at the same time.

Even with nothing connected to A0, you will see a voltage. What I measured when I did this experiment is shown in Figure 2.3.

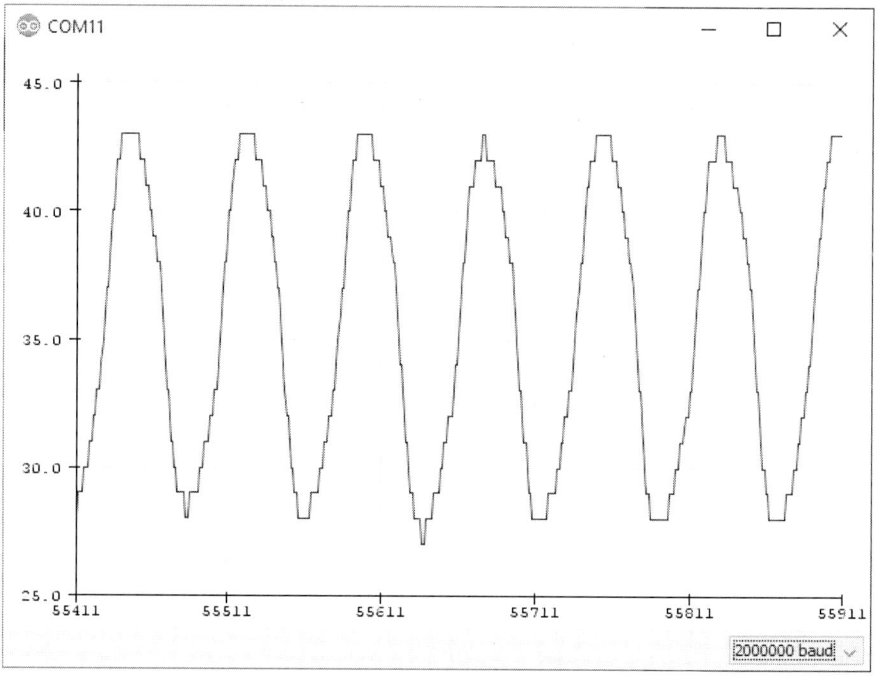

Figure 2.3. The voltage I measured on analog pin A0 with nothing connected and plotted on the serial plotter. Note the scale is in ADU from 0 to 1023

What do you think we are measuring? There is nothing connected to the ADC A0 pin.

Congratulations, you are measuring the 60 Hz pick up from stray electric fields in the room around you, radiating from all the power lines nearby. The power line voltage has a frequency of 60 Hz. This means there are 60 cycles of the voltage pattern every second.

The period of each complete cycle is 1/60 Hz or 16.67 msec. This is a good number to remember. The sine wave we see in this measurement has a period of 16.67 msec.

When we plug a sensor into the ADC pin that is low impedance, like a temperature sensor, a photo resistor, the 3.3 V reference voltage, even a flex sensor, the low resistance of the sensor will effectively short out the AC pick up and it will not be a problem except in extreme conditions. Don't worry about it for now.

2.4 Printing the time and the voltage

Many times, we will want to display the time at which the data was recorded and the voltage. This way we can plot data that varies with time on an x-y graph.

The simplest way of doing this is to use a timer as a counter and measure the time from the start of the sketch. We'll record the time in units of msec.

To the simple sketch to print the data, we will add the command to also print the time from the start of the sketch and print it out. When we do this, we cannot really plot on the serial plotter both the time and the voltage. If we try to do this, the scale will auto plot both curves and only one of them will be onscreen.

So, we will put the command to print the time on a separate line which we can comment out if we want to go back and plot the voltage on the serial plotter.

Here is the complete sketch:

```
void setup() {
  Serial.begin(2000000);
}
void loop() {
  Serial.print(millis());Serial.print(", ");
  Serial.println(analogRead(A0));
}
```

When this sketch runs, we will get two columns of data displayed on the serial monitor: the time from the start of the sketch, in msec, and the voltage, in units of the ADU levels from the ADC.

We can literally copy a segment of this screen to the clipboard and paste it into any spreadsheet, like excel. But, we need to use a special trick to turn the data pasted into the excel spreadsheet into two columns of data.

2.5 Plotting data in excel

To copy a large segment of data from the serial monitor, we first disable the auto scrolling by unclicking the box on the lower left of the screen. This is shown in Figure 2.4.

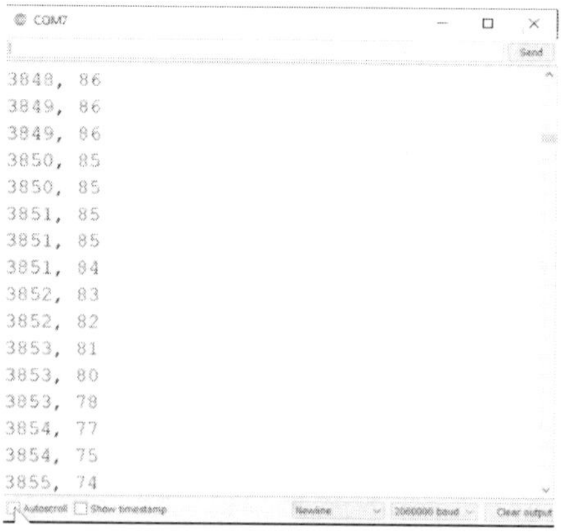

Figure 2.4. Screen shot of the serial monitor. Set the baud rate to 2000000 in the lower right of the screen and uncheck the auto scroll box on the lower left of the screen where the arrow points.

After we copy some of the serial monitor data to the clipboard, open up a blank spreadsheet and paste the data into a column. Excel will just think it is one column of data.

Now, select the column and under the Data menu, select the "Text to Columns" function. Use the delimiter feature and select commas and instantly, excel will transform your one column of text into two columns of data, ready to plot.

Now, you can select the two columns and insert the x-y plot. Instantly, you will see your data plotted. At this point, you can add axes and adjust the scales, and use either a line or keep the data as points. Figure 2.5 shows an example of a simple plot.

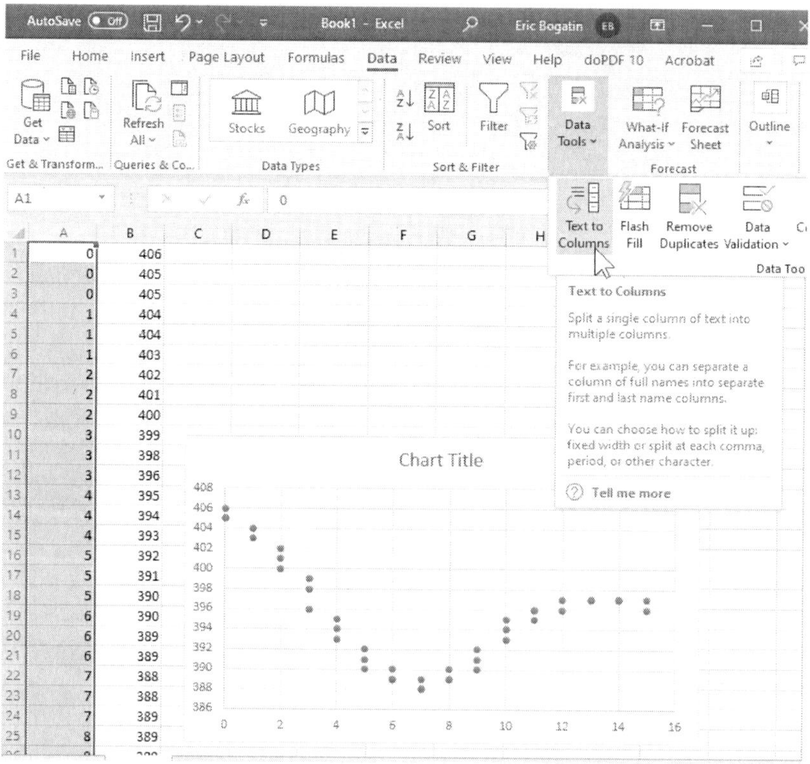

Figure 2.5. Excel sheet with the Text to Columns function highlighted. Note: a column of data has to be highlighted to use this feature. Select the two new columns and Insert x-y plot. The data is instantly plotted. From the Arduino to an excel plot in a few clicks.

Chapter 3. **Converting to Calibrated Voltage and Averaging**

Using these basic operations and all of seven lines of code in the sketch you can take data, plot it on the serial plotter, move it into excel and plot it using the excel data analysis functions.

The next step is to manipulate the data into a more interesting form and control when each point is measured.

3.1 Measuring a TMP36

Let's look at an interesting sensor. The first example is a TMP36 temperature sensor.

If you do not have one, you can purchase five of them here for about $4. The datasheet can be downloaded from here.

It has 3 pins sticking out the bottom. If you hold it with the pins facing you and the flat side up, the pin on the left is the 5 V pin, the one on the right is the gnd and the middle pin is the voltage that has the temperature information.

This is shown in Figure 3.1.

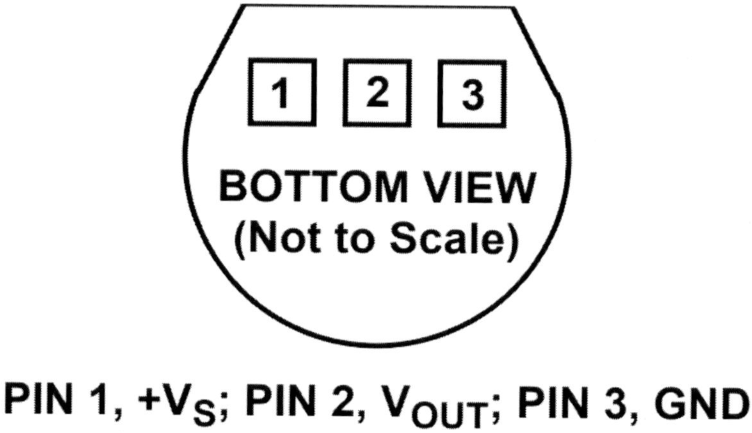

Figure 3.1. Pin diagram for the TMP36 taken from the datasheet.

Most online project guides will tell you to insert the sensor in a solderless breadboard (SBB), and connect wires to the 5 V pin, the gnd pin and the A0 pin.

We're not going to do that. Instead, we are going to do something far simpler. We are going to use a trick and make two of the analog pins become a power and ground pin and use another analog pin as an ADC pin.

Insert the TMP36 so the flat faces to the center of the board and the pins are sticking in the top three ADC pins. A TMP36 inserted into an Arduino Uno is shown in Figure 3.2.

Figure 3.2. TMP36 directly inserted into the analog pins. In this configuration, A0 should be gnd, A2 should be 5 V and A1 should be the ADC input.

In this orientation, we are going to make:

- ✓ *pin A0 0 V or a digital LOW*
- ✓ *pin A1 read by the ADC*
- ✓ *pin A2 a 5 V or a digital HIGH*

After we add the lines to set up the analog pins A0 and A2 as digital pins, we can literally use the sketch from the last chapter to read the ADC value which is the signal from the ADC pin A1, and print it with a time stamp.

Try this experiment: Print out the time and voltage measured with the temperature sensor connected, as digital levels from the ADC.

Here is my complete sketch:

```
int pinGND = A0;
int pin5V = A2;
int pinADC = A1;

void setup() {
  Serial.begin(2000000);
  pinMode (pinGND, OUTPUT);
  pinMode (pin5V, OUTPUT);
  digitalWrite (pinGND, LOW);
  digitalWrite (pin5V, HIGH);

}
void loop() {
  Serial.print(millis()); Serial.print(", ");
  Serial.println(analogRead(pinADC));
}
```

As you can see, I used variables to define which pins will be used for which function. This just makes the sketch a little more general.

The serial monitor will show two columns, the time from the start of the sketch, in msec, and the ADC value from the temperature sensor, in the digital levels from the ADC.

3.2 Processing the data

Now we are ready to do some real processing. We are going to:

- ✓ *Use variables to store the time and temperature values*

- ✓ *Calibrate the voltage values with the 3.3 V reference built into the Arduino board*
- ✓ *Convert the voltage into a temperature*
- ✓ *Control the time we print using a delay command*
- ✓ *Average the temperature measurements for some fixed number of samples*

We will use variables a lot going forward. If you are unfamiliar with variables, how to use them and how to name them, please check out the first book in the *Saturday Afternoon Low-Cost Electronics Projects* series, Arduinos Without Tears.

3.3 Storing ADC values in a variable in units of ADU

The analogRead () command returns a reading from the ADC channel. In the previous experiments, we just printed this out. We can also put this value in a variable and do more analysis with it.

While the level or count value from the ADC is just an integer and dimensionless, to remember that these integers came from an ADC and we are counting ADC levels, I add to the end of the variable name the generally accepted unit label of *Analog to Digital Units*, or ADUs.

For example, a variable storing an ADC value might be:

iADC_A0_ADU = analogRead(A0);

The way I decode the variable is:

- ✓ *The i means this variable is an integer*

- ✓ *The ADC_A0 means this variable is measuring what appears on the ADC A0 pin.*
- ✓ *The ADU means the units of this variable are analog to digital units, varying from 0 to 1023.*

Using variable names, we can write code that is a little more flexible. If we use variable names that are self-documenting, we can literally read the code and decipher what it does without needing a bunch of comment lines.

Should a reading from the ADC be stored as an integer or a floating-point number? The difference is an integer has no decimal point, but a floating-point number does have a decimal point.

When we are just going to use the raw ADU value from the ADC, using an integer value is just fine. In a few rare cases when we are limited in memory, using an int type will use the smallest memory. This will be the case in a future chapter when we want to store measurements into an array.

But, if we plan to do any averaging or more complex analysis, using integers will round-off any fractions and we would lose a little accuracy.

> ***If we plan to do any calculations with the ADU values, we should use the variable as a floating-point number. This will give us more accuracy.***

For example, if we use an int type variable to store the ADU value and measure the average of 1000 readings the average value will be rounded down to an integer value. We lose the fractional information, and the int type might be too small a number to store the large value of the running sum of 1000 measurements. This would cause an error when the int type number rolls over above 32000.

If the variable that stores the ADU values is a float type, we retain the fractional value of the average and can count really large numbers. This gives us a little more precision.

Generally, unless there is a strong compelling reason otherwise, I recommend using a float variable to store the ADC value. This gives us the most options.

For this experiment we really don't care what the actual voltage value is at the pin. Using the measurement in ADU units and displaying this is just fine for us right now.

Try this experiment: Read the voltage from the analog pin, place it into a float variable and print the variable along with the time. Use a delay so you print the voltage to the plotter every 20 msec.

Here is my sketch:

```
//initialize the variables at the beginning
float V_ADU;
int iDelay_msec = 20;

//set pin values for later
int pinGND = A0;
int pin5V = A2;
int pinADC = A1;

void setup() {
  //always use the higher baud rate that is stable
  Serial.begin(2000000);
  //set up the pins for the TMP36:
  pinMode (pinGND, OUTPUT);
  pinMode (pin5V, OUTPUT);
  digitalWrite (pinGND, LOW);
  digitalWrite (pin5V, HIGH);
}
void loop() {
  V_ADU = analogRead(pinADC) * 1.0;
  Serial.print(millis()); Serial.print(", ");
  Serial.println(V_ADU);
```

```
  // use a delay to control the sample rate
  delay(iDelay_msec);
}
```

We are controlling the time interval for each point with the delay command. When we print out the data on the serial monitor, we get the two columns of time and ADC reading.

If we want to plot the ADC readings on the serial plotter, we have to comment out the line where we print the time column using the two slashes: //.

With 20 msec between measurements and 500 measurements full scale, this is 0.02 sec x 500 = 10 seconds full scale. This is a convenient time scale to watch the data scroll by.

What do you see? My initial measurement, after touching the temperature sensor, is shown in Figure 3.3.

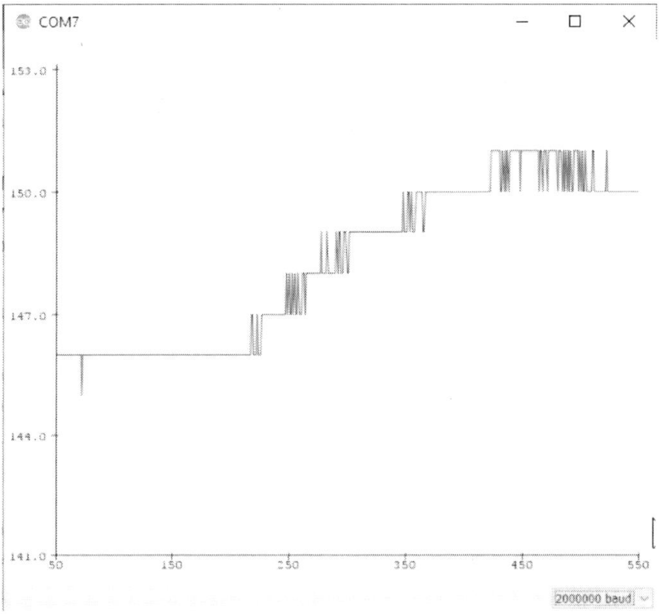

Figure 3.3. A snippet from the temperature sensor ADC reading after touching the sensor. You can see the individual discrete levels of the 10-bit ADC.

The time between data points is spaced 20 msec. This is a sample rate of 1/0.02 Samples/sec = 50 S/sec and with 500 points full scale on the serial plotter, 500 points x 0.02 sec/point = 10 sec full scale in one screen.

3.4 Simple conversion of ADU to Volts

When displaying a voltage that I will plot on the serial plotter, I prefer using units of mV instead of volts. This is due to the auto scaling of the plotter.

The smallest units per division on the vertical scale are 3 units per division, with 4 divisions full scale. This means the highest resolution scale is 12 units full scale.

If we use units of volts, we can only plot 12 Volts full scale. Our entire measured voltage range is only 0 V to 5 V, so this is less than half the screen. Typically, if we are looking at small voltage changes we will never see them on this scale.

In order to plot larger numbers and take advantage of the auto scaling limits, we can use milliVolts (mV) and be able to see smaller voltage changes on the screen.

We can quickly convert the measured voltage in ADU units into a voltage, in mV, if we multiply the ADU value by the conversion factor, 5000.0 mV/1023 ADU.

One way to quickly see how to create a conversion factor is to just look at the units:

ADU x mV/ADU = mV

The ADU units cancel out and we are left with just mV.

This is a quick, handy way of figuring out conversion factors. Look at the units and what terms need to be in the numerator or denominator to get the units to come out the way you want. This is one reason I like to use ADU units as a place holder.

I add the decimal point to 5000 so that it is a floating-point number and the calculation is done as floating-point.

We can check the accuracy of the ADC by comparing its measurement with a reference voltage of known value.

Built into every Arduino board is a 3.3 V Low-Drop-Out (LDO) regulator. It is specified as 3.30 V to 1% accuracy. I've verified this using a DMM accurate to better than 0.1%.

We can measure the 3.3 v power rail on the Arduino board using this basic conversion factor. I connected the ADC pin A5 to the 3.3 V rail.

My complete sketch, including the code to set up the TMP36, is here:

```
float V_ADU;
float V_mV;
// using a basic low accuracy conversion factor
float mV_per_ADU = 5000.0 / 1023;

int iDelay_msec = 20;
int pinGND = A0;
int pin5V = A2;
//connect the A5 pin to the 3.3 V rail
int pinADC = A5;

void setup() {
  Serial.begin(2000000);
  pinMode (pinGND, OUTPUT);
  pinMode (pin5V, OUTPUT);
  digitalWrite (pinGND, LOW);
  digitalWrite (pin5V, HIGH);
}
void loop() {
// take the actual measurement:
  V_ADU = analogRead(pinADC) * 1.0;

// convert it to mV:
  V_mV = V_ADU * mV_per_ADU;
  Serial.print(millis()); Serial.print(", ");
  Serial.print(V_ADU); Serial.print(", ");
  Serial.println(V_mV);
  delay(iDelay_msec);
}
```

Using this sketch, I measured a voltage on the 3.3 V rail as 3,225 mV. This is off from 3,300 mV by 75 m V/3,300 mV = 2.2%. If this level of accuracy is good enough, no further calibration is necessary.

3.5 Using the 3.3 V rail to calibrate the ADC

If you want 1% accuracy, here is a trick you can do. When we use the ADC to measure the 3.3 V rail, we can use the ADU value we measure to generate a new scale factor. In my sketch above, the ADU value was printed along with the simple calibrated value in mV. In this example, I measured a value of 660 ADU for the 3.3 V reference voltage.

If we assume a simple calibration curve of 0 V in = 0 ADU and 3300 mV in = 660 ADU, then the new scale factor is:

3300 mV/value_ADU = 3300/660.

There is no need to even divide this out. We can let the Arduino do it for us. Afterall, it's always important to remember, ***computers work for us, we don't work for computers***.

At the beginning of the sketch we change the conversion factor, mV_per_ADU, to:

```
float mV_per_ADU=3300.0/660;
```

We multiply each measured ADC value, in ADU, by this conversion factor.

Now, when we run the code, and display the ADC value in units of ADU, multiply it by the new calibrated scale factor and the new value in milliVolts is a better calibration of the voltage at the input to the ADC.

When you run this modified sketch, you will see it reads, 3300 mV, exactly as expected.

Of course, in your sketch, use the value of the ADU reading when you measure the 3.3 V rail on your Arduino board.

This is the calibration factor for the ADC. All channels use the same ADC so all channels will be calibrated to within a 1% absolute accuracy using this method.

When we read the A1 channel with the ADC, we will literally read the voltage on the sensor, which is related to the temperature.

I adjusted the delay to be 100 msec between points so that it takes about 500 points x 0.1 second/point = 50 seconds to display on the full screen.

When this sketch runs, the voltage, in mV, we start at is about 730 mV. This is the voltage of the temperature sensor at room temperature. I then touched it to raise its temperature, then let it fall. The first 50 seconds of voltage measurements on the TMP36 temperature sensor are shown in Figure 3.4.

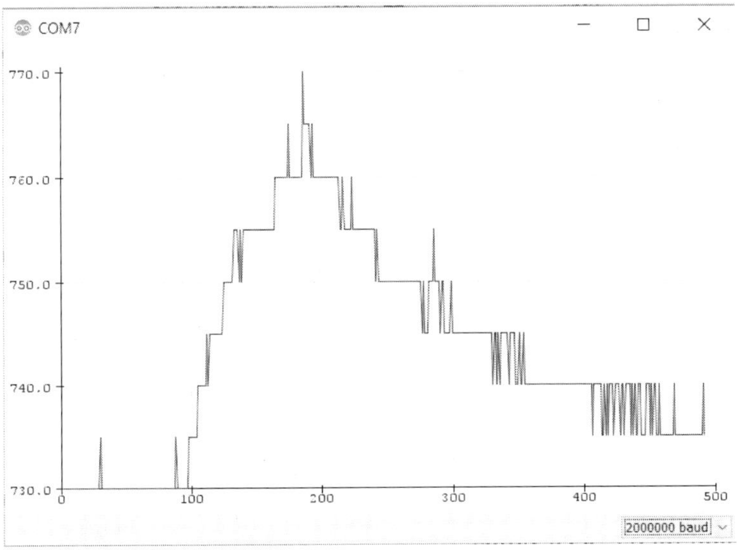

Figure 3.4. Temperature sensor recorded at 50 sec full scale and in calibrated mV on the vertical scale.

3.6 Converting voltage to temperature

As the next step, we can convert this voltage into a temperature using the simple conversion term, based on the datasheet:

Temp_degC = V_mV/10.0 – 50.0

We can convert this into degrees F with:

Temp_degF = Temp_degC x 9/5 + 32

The temperature I measured initially was about 73 degF. I touched the sensor with my finger, then let go and watched the temperature increase a few degrees and drop back down during the first 50 sec. This response is shown in Figure 3.5.

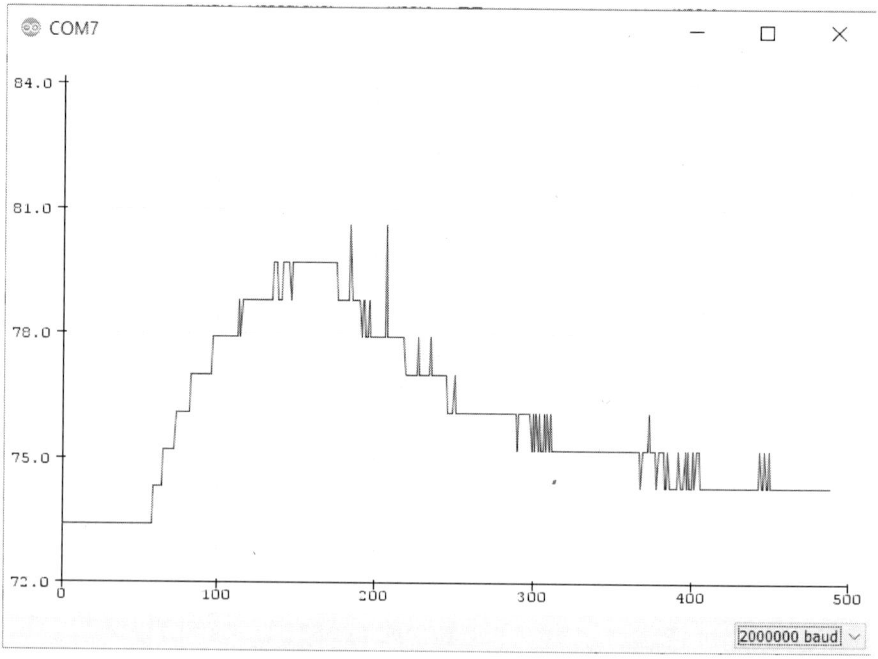

Figure 3.5. The output of this sketch showing the response of the temperature sensor to my touch. Note in auto-scale, there are 3 degF per division. This is the highest resolution we can plot in the serial plotter.

While the voltage recorded is calibrated to about 1% absolute accuracy, the temperature is not this accurate. The data sheet for the TMP36 says the absolute accuracy is within +/- 2 degC, which is about +/- 3.6 degF.

3.7 Averaging n points

So far, the way we controlled the sample rate was with a delay. This is very inefficient. We are leaving data on the table that we could be using to get an average.

Calculating an average value means adding up a bunch of consecutive values and then dividing by the number of samples. We do this in a *for loop*.

We introduce the new variable, npts_ave as the number of points we average. The more points, the longer it takes for each averaged value to record. This will slow the plotting time down.

If you are not familiar with for loops, be sure to check out the first book in the *Saturday Afternoon Low-Cost Electronics Projects* series, Arduinos Without Tears.

The sketch to average some number of consecutive recordings and display the averaged, calibrated temperature is really easy to create from where we ended up. By using a value of about npts_ave = 1000, the measurement interval is about 0.1 sec.

Here is my complete sketch:

```
// initialize the variables
int npts_ave = 1000;// number of points to average
float V_ADU;
float V_mV;     // to store the voltage measurements
float mV_per_ADU = 3300.0 / 660;

float Temp_degC; // to store the temperature values
float Temp_degF;
```

```
int iDelay_msec = 100;
int pinGND = A0;
int pin5V = A2;
int pinADC = A1;

void setup() {
  Serial.begin(2000000);
  pinMode (pinGND, OUTPUT);
  pinMode (pin5V, OUTPUT);
  digitalWrite (pinGND, LOW);
  digitalWrite (pin5V, HIGH);
}
void loop() {

  V_ADU = 0.0; // initialize running sum to 0

  // take and add up the npts_ave measurements
  for (int i = 1; i <= npts_ave; i++) {
    V_ADU = V_ADU + analogRead(pinADC) * 1.0;
  }

  V_ADU = V_ADU / npts_ave;     // get the average
  V_mV = V_ADU * mV_per_ADU;   // convert to voltage
  Temp_degC = V_mV / 10.0 - 50.0;
  Temp_degF = Temp_degC * 9 / 5 + 32;

// print out the values
// manually comment in or out the lines to print
  Serial.print(millis()); Serial.print(", ");
  //Serial.print(V_ADU); Serial.print(", ");
  //Serial.println(V_mV);
  //Serial.println(Temp_degC);
  Serial.println(Temp_degF);
// note: last line is a println to add return at end
}
```

The output of this sketch, displayed on the serial monitor, is shown in Figure 3.6.

```
COM7

119, 73.49
241, 73.47
362, 73.48
483, 73.47
604, 73.49
724, 73.50
846, 73.47
967, 73.47
1088, 73.49
1209, 73.47
1330, 73.51
1452, 73.48
1572, 73.50
1693, 73.48
```

Figure 3.6. The output from the temperature measurements with an average of 1000 consecutive measurements. The first column is the time in msec and the second is the temperature in degF.

The time interval between displayed values is 112 msec. This is how long it takes to make 1000 measurements. This suggests the time per measurement is 112 msec/1000 = 112 usec per acquisition.

After commenting out the line for printing the time, the measurements on the serial plotter for the temperature in degF, are shown in Figure 3.7. This shows the measurements after I touched the temperature sensor.

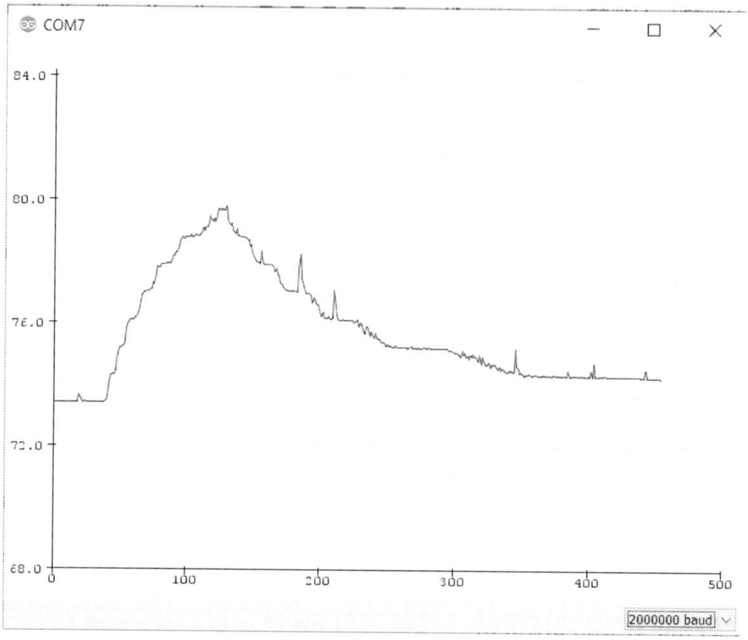

Figure 3.7. Measured temperature displayed in degF with 1000 points averaged per point. Horizontal time base is 50 sec full scale. Vertical scale is temperature in degF.

Averaging 1000 consecutive points has decreased the noise level, but does not really change the voltage resolution which translated into the temperature resolution. Only a higher bit resolution will do this, which we introduce in a later chapter.

Chapter 4. Pushing the Limits of the Built in ADC

So far, we have used the ADC in a very simple way. We took a reading, converted it into a voltage or a temperature, averaged it a little and printed it out or plotted it. There're a few more improvements we can make with this built-in ADC that will push it to its limits.

In particular we will:

- ✓ *Speed up the sample rate*
- ✓ *Record the data into an array and plot it to the screen like an oscilloscope*
- ✓ *Average for a fixed period of time and display as a scope or as a strip chart recorder*
- ✓ *Print the time and voltage measured for each averaged point*
- ✓ *Print the data to a text file*
- ✓ *Print the data directly into an excel file and plot in excel*

4.1 Measure sample rate for the built in ADC analogRead function

If we were to take measurements from the ADC as fast as possible, just how fast is this? The previous sketch actually measured this. We measured the time to recorded 1000 points as 112 msec. We can formalize this process of measuring the time for any acquisition by recording how long it takes to execute a large number of points and divide the total time interval by the number of samples. This can be implemented in a simple *for loop*.

For example, the algorithm might be:

- ✓ *Start a stopwatch*
- ✓ *Take 10,000 measurements*
- ✓ *Stop the stopwatch*
- ✓ *Take the elapsed time and divide by 10,000*

Using this algorithm, we can measure the execution time of any process.

The sketch to use this method to measure the time to take an ADC reading is the following:

```
// set up all the initial variables
int npts_ave = 10000;
float V_ADU;
float V_mV;
float mV_per_ADU = 3300.0 / 660;

float Temp_degC;
float Temp_degF;

int iDelay_msec = 100;
int pinGND = A0;
int pin5V = A2;
int pinADC = A1;
long iTime_start_usec;
float Time_X_usec;

void setup() {
  Serial.begin(2000000);
  pinMode (pinGND, OUTPUT);
  pinMode (pin5V, OUTPUT);
  digitalWrite (pinGND, LOW);
  digitalWrite (pin5V, HIGH);
}
void loop() {
```

```
  V_ADU = 0.0;
  iTime_start_usec = micros(); // start the timer
  for (int i = 1; i <= npts_ave; i++) {
    //V_ADU = V_ADU + analogRead(pinADC) * 1.0; // use later
    analogRead(pinADC);       // just read the ADC, fastest possible
    // note: a comment takes no extra time in the loop
  }
  Time_X_usec = (micros() - iTime_start_usec * 1.0) / npts_ave;
  // stop the timer, measure the difference, take the average
  //Time_X_usec is the execution time in usec for the operation

  V_ADU = V_ADU / npts_ave;
  V_mV = V_ADU * mV_per_ADU;
  Temp_degC = V_mV / 10.0 - 50.0;
  Temp_degF = Temp_degC * 9 / 5 + 32;
  //Serial.print(millis()); Serial.print(", ");
  //Serial.print(V_ADU); Serial.print(", ");
  //Serial.println(V_mV);
  //Serial.println(Temp_degC);
  //Serial.println(Temp_degF);
  Serial.println(Time_X_usec); // print out the execution time
}
```

When I ran this on my Arduino Uno, I measured a time to take one measurement as 112 usec. This is a sample rate, when running flat out, of 1/112 usec = 8,900 Samples/sec or 8.9 kS/sec.

Using a simple to install library, we can speed this up by over a factor of 7.

4.2 Using the faster sampling library

There is a library available which has a slightly different driver for the Atmega 328 microcontroller to reduce the delays in reading a measurement from the ADC.

The library can be installed using the built-in library feature in the Arduino IDE. Just go to Sketch/Include Library/Library manager. This is shown in Figure 4.1. If you are not familiar with this process, check out the second book in the *Saturday Afternoon*

Low-Cost Electronics series, Science Experiments with Arduinos using a Multi-Function Board.

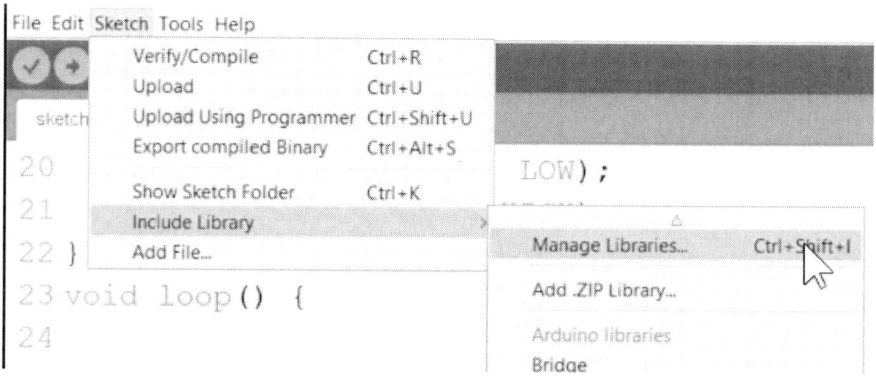

Figure 4.1. Open up the library manager from Sketch/Include Library/Manage libraries.

When the screen opens up, search for "fast adc" and you will pull up two libraries. Select the second library, avdweb_AnalogReadFast by Albert van Dalen. This is shown in Figure 4.2. Click the install button and you are ready to go. You can read about this library from Albert's web site here.

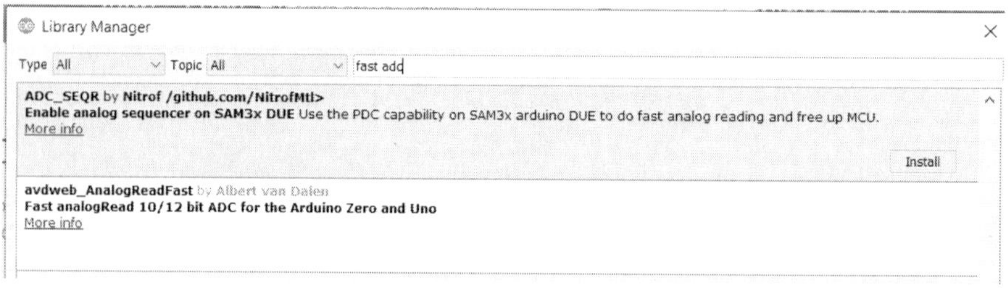

Figure 4.2. Search for "fast ADC" and you will find the library to speed up the ADC readings. Choose the bottom one that has already been installed.

Using this library is really simple. All we have to do is add, at the beginning of the sketch, the include statement:

#include <avdweb_AnalogReadFast.h>

Then, instead of using the analogRead() command, we use a new command which is part of this library, analogReadFast(adcPin).

Here is the complete sketch to measure the acquisition speed of the ADC using this new library command:

```
#include <avdweb_AnalogReadFast.h> // must be at top

int npts_ave = 10000;
float V_ADU;
float V_mV;
float mV_per_ADU = 3300.0 / 660;

float Temp_degC;
float Temp_degF;

int iDelay_msec = 100;
int pinGND = A0;
int pin5V = A2;
int pinADC = A1;
long iTime_start_usec;
float Time_X_usec;

void setup() {
  Serial.begin(2000000);
  pinMode (pinGND, OUTPUT);
  pinMode (pin5V, OUTPUT);
  digitalWrite (pinGND, LOW);
  digitalWrite (pin5V, HIGH);
}
void loop() {

  V_ADU = 0.0;
  iTime_start_usec = micros();
  for (int i = 1; i <= npts_ave; i++) {
    //V_ADU = V_ADU + analogReadFast(pinADC) * 1.0;

  // add the analogReadFast command here:
    analogReadFast(pinADC);
  }
  Time_X_usec = (micros() - iTime_start_usec * 1.0);
  Time_X_usec = Time_X_usec / npts_ave;
```

```
  V_ADU = V_ADU / npts_ave;
  V_mV = V_ADU * mV_per_ADU;
  Temp_degC = V_mV / 10.0 - 50.0;
  Temp_degF = Temp_degC * 9 / 5 + 32;
  //Serial.print(millis()); Serial.print(", ");
  //Serial.print(V_ADU); Serial.print(", ");
  //Serial.println(V_mV);
  //Serial.println(Temp_degC);
  //Serial.println(Temp_degF);

  Serial.println(Time_X_usec);
  // print the execution time for the fast read
}
```

When it runs on my Arduino Uno, I recorded a time interval between samples of 15.28 usec. This is a sample rate of 1/15.28 usec = 65 kS/sec. It was 112 usec using the standard analogRead() command. Using the faster read command, the fastest sample rate speeded up from 8.9 kS/sec to 65 kS/sec, or an increase by a factor of 7.3x.

Going forward, we should always use this faster sampling rate. Why not?

4.3 Using an Arduino as an Oscilloscope

If we want to take measurements as fast as we can and immediately display the measurement, we could take a reading, print it and go to the next measurement.

If we do this, it takes longer than 15.28 usec because we have to send the data over the serial port. This wastes time, even using the highest baud rate of 2000000.

If we want a faster measurement rate, but still display the data, we should write each measurement into an array and then print the array after we have collected all the data.

The algorithm is to:

- ✓ *Initialize the array*
- ✓ *Use a for loop to read 500 measurements*
- ✓ *In each iteration, read the ADC value and immediately write it into an array element*
- ✓ *Continue the loop*
- ✓ *After taking 500 points, use another loop to print them to the serial plotter.*
- ✓ *Wait a little to see the data and repeat.*

When we use arrays with the Arduino Uno, we have to be careful about the size of the array. The Uno is very limited in memory. It is not really designed for sophisticated data acquisition.

A more serious data acquisition Arduino is one based on the SAMD51 microcontroller. It has more memory, a faster clock and higher resolution ADC plus two true DAC outputs. This device is detailed in Book 5 in the Saturday Afternoon Low-Cost Electronics Projects series.

In the Uno, we are limited in how large an array we can create and use. An int type number takes up 2 bytes and is the smallest type of number. If we want to use an array as large as 501 points, so the contents just fills s serial plotter screen, we can only save the data as an int type.

If we use a float-type or long array, we are limited to an array size of less than about 301 points before we get low memory warnings.

A float-type and long integer type number both take the same amount of memory. If we use either type, the largest array size we can use is about 301 points. This has an important consequence when we want to use a 16-bit ADC.

If we use an int type, which takes less memory per point, we can create an array as large as 601 points before we start getting low memory and stability warnings.

This means that we can at least record 501 points using the int type for the array. I left the averaging feature inside the sketch. When we set it to 1 average, it will just take data as quickly as possible.

Here is my sketch that implements this simple algorithm:

```
#include <avdweb_AnalogReadFast.h>
int npts_ave = 1; // number of averages per point
const long npts_arr = 501;
// use a constant type so it will work as an array
dimension

int arrV_ADU[npts_arr];
// I define an array variable with arr at beginning

float V_ADU;
float V_mV;
float mV_per_ADU = 3300.0 / 660;

float Temp_degC;
float Temp_degF;

int iDelay_msec = 100;
int pinGND = A0;
int pin5V = A2;
int pinADC = A1;
long iTime_start_usec;
float Time_X_usec;

void setup() {
  Serial.begin(2000000);
  pinMode (pinGND, OUTPUT);
  pinMode (pin5V, OUTPUT);
```

```
  digitalWrite (pinGND, LOW);
  digitalWrite (pin5V, HIGH);
}
void loop() {
  //initialize the array for the running sum
  for (int j = 1; j < npts_arr; j++) {
    arrV_ADU[j] = 0.0;
  }

  iTime_start_usec = micros(); // start timer
  for (int j = 1; j < npts_arr; j++) {
    // do averages per point
    for (int i = 1; i <= npts_ave; i++) {
      arrV_ADU[j] = arrV_ADU[j] + analogReadFast(pinADC);
    }
    //done with averages
  }
  // done with filling the array of 500 points

  Time_X_usec = (micros() - iTime_start_usec * 1.0);
  Time_X_usec = Time_X_usec / (npts_arr - 1);
  // acquisition time for each data point in array
  // note: the array just has the raw ADU sums

  //now to scale and print out the array
  for (int j = 1; j < npts_arr; j++) {
    V_ADU = arrV_ADU[j]; // suck out each point
    V_ADU = V_ADU / npts_ave; // average it
    V_mV = V_ADU * mV_per_ADU; // convert to voltage
    Temp_degC = V_mV / 10.0 - 50.0;
    Temp_degF = Temp_degC * 9 / 5 + 32;

    // select which terms and in what order to print
    // to print one number on serial plotter use .println

    //Serial.print(millis()); Serial.print(", ");
    //Serial.print(V_ADU); Serial.print(", ");
    //Serial.println(V_mV);
    //Serial.println(Temp_degC);
    Serial.println(Temp_degF);
    //Serial.println(Time_X_usec);
  }
  delay(2000);  // add delay to pause the screen
}
```

This sketch is set up to measure the execution time to take 501 measurements as fast as possible and display them on screen at a time, just like an oscilloscope.

On my Arduino Uno, I measured 16.02 usec per acquisition. The acquisition time for just accessing the ADC was 15.28 usec.

Adding the writing to the array, the additional execution time is 0.74 usec. The clock is 16 MHz. This additional time is 16 MHz x 0.74 usec = ~ 12 clock cycles. This is the additional time to write into an array, well worth the time.

When we acquire measurements at this faster rate, and print 500 points on the serial plotter, the total time this represents is 500 x 16 usec = 8 msec. This is about half of a power line cycle, which has a period of about 16 msec. We should see a fraction of a cycle when we plot one buffer of measurements while measuring just the 60 Hz pick up.

Sure enough, when I display the signal from ADC pin A4, just left open, which picks up the stray 60 Hz, I see a fraction of a cycle. If I replace the analogReadFast() command with the default analogRead() command, the slower analogRead function, I see 0.112 msec/point x 500 points = 55 msec or about 3 cycles of the 60 Hz pick up noise. This comparison is shown in Figure 4.3.

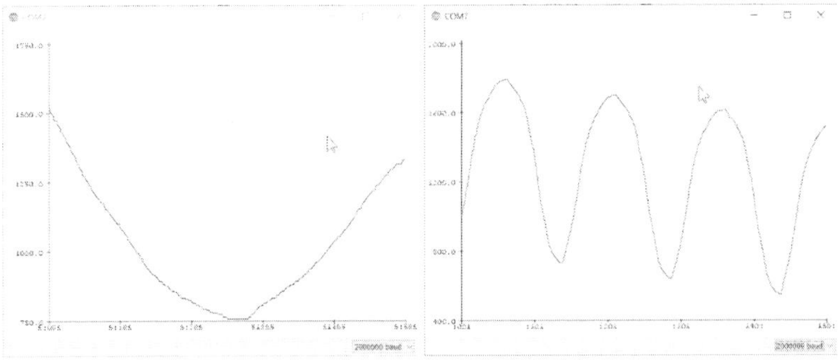

Figure 4.3. Measurements of 60 Hz pick up on analog pin A4 using the fast analog read command on the left and the default, slow analog read on the right. Each power line cycle is about 16.7 msec long.

By adding a delay after the 500-point buffer is printed out, we have time to look at the data, or copy and paste the data into excel.

This process we implemented- take data as fast as we can, store it in an array and print in out when we are done- is basically an oscilloscope. We can roughly control the length of the time base plotted by changing the number of averages we take per recorded point.

For this Arduino Uno, we take data at about 62 kS/sec or a buffer size of 8 msec full scale at the fastest rate. If we average for 2 points, it takes about 16 msec full scale. Using an average of 3 consecutive measurements per point and we have 24 msec full scale.

4.4 Looking at a PWM signal

As a simple example of this scope, we can measure the signal from a pulse width modulated (PWM) pin. There are two different frequencies. On the Arduino, pins 5 and 6 run at 980 Hz, while the other PWM pins operate at 490 Hz.

At 490 Hz, and 8 msec full scale, we should see a total of 490 Hz x 0.008 sec = 3.92 cycles.

In this example, we set pin 9 as the PWM signal and use the analogWrite(9,128) command to write an 8-bit number with a value of 128. This is a duty cycle of 128/512 = 50%. A value of 10 means a very small duty cycle and a value of 200 means a very large duty cycle. The scope traces from the serial plotter for these three conditions are shown in Figure 4.4.

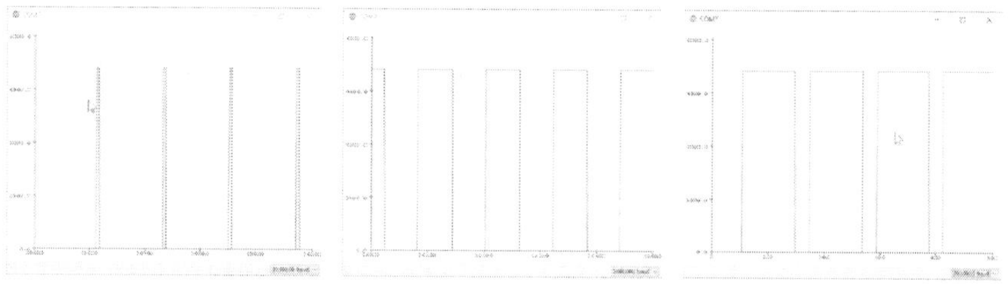

Figure 4.4. Measured PWM signal using the scope function at 8 msec full scale for three different PWM settings, 10, 128 and 200.

4.5 How good of a sine wave can be measured?

To verify the accuracy of the ADC readings, I used a function generator that is part of the Digilent Analog Discovery 2 scope to generate a sine wave with a frequency of 1 kHz.

With a full screen time base of 8 msec, this will give about 8 cycles in one screen image. I printed 500 points from the ADC to the serial monitor, copied this to my clipboard and pasted it and the time per point into an excel spreadsheet. I then synthesized an ideal sine wave based on the settings for the sine wave generated by the function generator.

I plotted the measured voltages and the synthesized voltages on a graph. This is shown in Figure 4.5 is an example of the measured recording of the 1 kHz sine wave with an amplitude of 2 V and offset of 2.2 V, compared to that of an ideal sine wave.

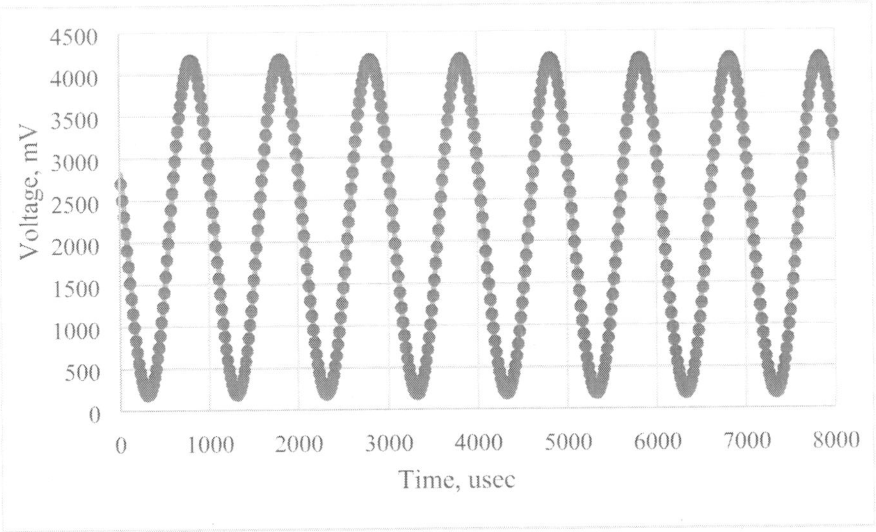

Figure 4.5. Measured voltage (dots) and simulated voltage of an ideal sine wave (line).

In this example, an ideal sine wave was simulated based on the simple model of:

V(t) = offset + amplitude x sin(2π x time x frequency + phase)

For this analysis, I used the dead reckoning values of:

- ✓ *Offset = 2200 mV*
- ✓ *Amplitude = 2000 mV*
- ✓ *Frequency = 1 kHz*
- ✓ *Time = 16.04 usec x index*

I've done some analysis of the quality of this sine wave generator and found it to produce an ideal sine wave to better than 0.1% accuracy. This is roughly a 2 mV residual error out of an amplitude of 2000 mV.

To get the good match between what was measured by the ADC and what was simulated for an ideal sine wave, all I adjusted was the initial phase. Since there is no synchronization between when the ADC starts taking data and the generated sine wave, this initial phase will be different every time the sine wave is measured.

In this particular case, I used a value of the initial phase of 0.434 cycles to get this agreement. When the simulated and measured curves are within the pen width of the plots, it helps to look at the residuals. This is the difference between the measured and simulated voltages at each time instant. The units for the difference will be mV. Figure 4.6 shows an example of the best-case residual difference, for the optimized phase.

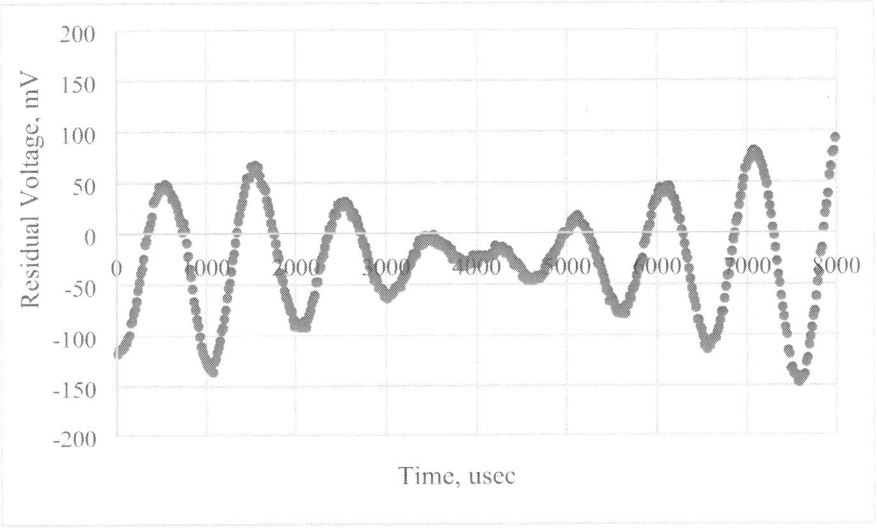

Figure 4.6. The residual difference between the measured and simulated sine wave after optimizing just the initial phase.

This says that the inherent absolute accuracy of the ADC is pretty good, but could be improved. For example, the offset can be adjusted by about 22 mV.

The absolute calibration is good to 1%. Out of an amplitude of 2000 mV, 1% is 20 mV. This is about what the offset is off.

The funny shape of the residual error waveform is probably due to a slight drift in the time base of the ADC sampling. It could also be related to a slight frequency drift of the sine wave source. This is the best we can match using an ideal sine wave.

As it is, the match is to within 50 mV residual amplitude error out of 2000 mV amplitude. This is about 2.5% absolute error.

4.6 Averaging for a fixed amount of time

So far, we've taken a fixed number of measurements in an average, converted the ADU value into a voltage, and either printed the result or plotted the result on the screen.

This is the scope mode of operation.

Instead of averaging for a fixed number of points, we will average for a fixed time interval. Since this time interval will generally by more than a few millisec, rather than use the scope mode of operation, we'll use the stripchart mode of operation: display each point as it comes out.

To maintain a high level of accuracy for the averaging time, I will define the averaging time in msec, but convert this to usec when I calculate the time interval over which to average.

Here is the algorithm we can use to record measurements over a fixed time interval and average them together to end up with one value:

1. *Define a time interval over which to average*
2. *Start a timer*
3. *Take a measurement and add it to the previous ones, as a running sum*
4. *Use a counter to keep track of the number of acquisitions over the interval*
5. *Keep taking data and adding them to the running sum*

6. *When the time interval has reached its limit, stop taking the measurements*
7. *Divide the running sum by the number of points taken*
8. *Record the time since the start of the sketch minus half the acquisition time*
9. *Print out the time for the point and its value*
10. *Or plot the average value.*
11. *Start over again*

Here is the void loop() part of my sketch to implement this algorithm.

```
void loop() {
 V_ADU = 0.0;
  iCounter1 = 0;// use this to count number of points in average
  iTime_stop_usec = micros() + iTime_ave_usec; // when to stop

  while (micros() < iTime_stop_usec) {
    V_ADU = V_ADU + analogReadFast(pinADC); // collect running sum
    iCounter1++;
  }
// done, ready to find average value

  V_ADU = V_ADU / iCounter1;

  V_mV = V_ADU * mV_per_ADU;
  Time_point_sec = ((micros() - 0.5 * iTime_ave_usec))*1.0e-6;

// just print to serial monitor for now
  Serial.print(iCounter1); Serial.print(", ");
  Serial.print(Time_point_sec); Serial.print(", ");
  Serial.println(V_mV);
}
```

In this sketch we are calculating the average one point at a time and plotting the average value as a running value.

Within the acquisition loop, we want to do the minimum calculations so we don't take time from the measurements.

When I used an averaging time of 100 msec, I found there were 3000 samples acquired in each 100 msec time interval. This is a time per point of 100,000 usec/3000 points = 33 usec per point. This is about twice as slow in the while loop than in the for loop.

4.7 Averaging for n power line cycles

What's a good averaging time?

In many measurements, it is common to find some 60 Hz pick up. Of course, the first step is to minimize this by using a low input resistance source, reducing the length of antennas, keeping power cords far away and doing some shielding. After we've done all of this, we can still reduce the 60 Hz pick up using digital filtering.

This trick will dramatically reduce the 60 Hz pick up by averaging over an integral number of cycles. Any noise that is periodic with the averaging time will be averaged to zero.

The cycle time for 60 Hz is called a power line cycle, PLC. The trick is to use an averaging time that is an integer number of 1 PLC. If we do this, the 60 Hz noise is dramatically reduced.

One PLC is 1/60 sec = 16.67 msec. We select the number of power line cycles to average over, nPLC and use this to define the averaging time:

averaging interval = Time_ave_usec = nPLC/60.0 *1e6

To provide the option of using a hardcoded value for the averaging time or using nPLC, I added an if statement to look at the nPLC value. If it is 0, then use the hardcoded value of the averaging time.

If it is other than 0, then use the averaging time based on the nPLC value:

```
if (nPLC!=0){iTime_ave_usec=(nPLC/60.0)*1.0e6;}
```

The complete sketch is here:

```
#include <avdweb_AnalogReadFast.h>

//scope:
int npts_ave = 1;
const long npts_arr = 501;
int arrV_ADU[npts_arr];
float Time_X_usec;

//stripchart recorder:
long iTime_ave_usec = 1000;
int nPLC = 6; //set to 0 for hard coded averaging
long iTime_stop_usec;
long iCounter1;
long iTime_start_usec;

//general measurements:
float V_ADU;
float V_mV;
float mV_per_ADU = 3300.0 / 660;
float Time_point_sec;

//temp sensor:
float Temp_degC;
float Temp_degF;
int pinGND = A0;
int pin5V = A2;
int pinADC = A4;

void setup() {
  Serial.begin(2000000);
  pinMode (pinGND, OUTPUT);
  pinMode (pin5V, OUTPUT);
  digitalWrite (pinGND, LOW);
  digitalWrite (pin5V, HIGH);
  analogWrite(9, 200);

// set time ot average based on nPLC
  if (nPLC != 0) {
    iTime_ave_usec = (nPLC / 60.0) * 1.0e6;
// do the calculation as floating, but use the long value
  }
}
```

```
void loop() {
  V_ADU = 0.0;
  iCounter1 = 0;
// calculate the time to stop this measurement point
  iTime_stop_usec = micros() + iTime_ave_usec;
  while (micros() < iTime_stop_usec) {
    V_ADU = V_ADU + analogReadFast(pinADC); // running sum
    iCounter1++;
  }
// data collection complete, now to find average value
  V_ADU = V_ADU / iCounter1;

  V_mV = V_ADU * mV_per_ADU;
  Time_point_sec = ((micros() - 0.5 * iTime_ave_usec)) * 1.0e-6;
  Temp_degC = V_mV / 10.0 - 50.0;
  Temp_degF = Temp_degC * 9 / 5 + 32;

// select what to print on serial monitor or plotter
  //Serial.print(iCounter1); Serial.print(", ");
  //Serial.print(Time_point_sec, 3); Serial.print(", ");
  Serial.print(100); Serial.print(", "); // adjusts plotter scale
  Serial.println(V_mV);
}
```

I added one special feature so we can fix the scale. Normally, the serial plotter will autoscale the screen to fit all the plotted data on the screen at one time.

When I want to fix the scales so I can compare one curve with another on exactly the same scales, I plot a dummy number as a curve which sets the upper scale. This is the line: Serial.print(100);

When we look at just an open ADC pin and see 60 Hz pick up, you can see the difference between using some time interval, like 10 msec and a time interval like nPLC = 1. This is shown in Figure 4.7.

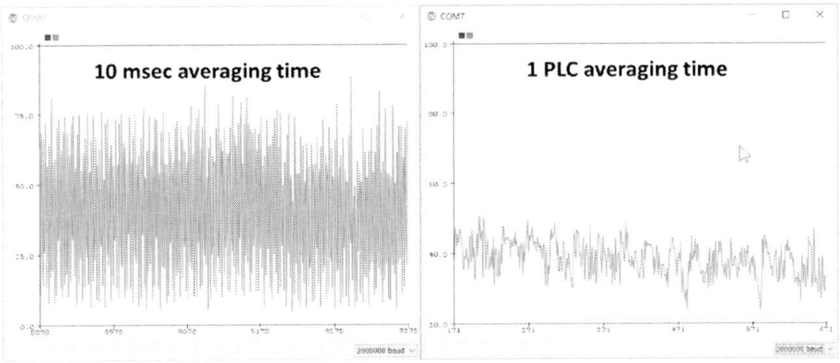

Figure 4.7. The measured voltage with an integral number of power line cycles averaged, compared to a 10 msec averaging. Note the reduction in noise is down to less than 20 mV peak to peak.

If you are going to average for more than 10 msec per point, its good practice to use some number of PLC. Here is a handy table of the nPLC value and the averaging time per point:

nPLC	time
1	*16.67 msec*
2	*33.3 msec*
3	*50 msec*
4	*66.7 msec*
5	*83.3 msec*
6	*100 msec*
9	*150 msec*
12	*200 msec*
18	*300 msec*
30	*500 msec*
60	*1 sec*

4.8 Using functions

We've increased the complexity of our sketches enough and added enough options that it is time to introduce using functions to simplify and clean up the code.

A function is a piece of code that we can call by shouting out its name and it runs. Functions are also called subroutines in some other languages. We write the algorithm we want to run in a function, with an entry and exit point, and can call it over and over again.

We define the function in a separate location in the code, usually after the void loop() command.

In fact, once we see the structure of a function, it will be clear that the void setup() and the void loop() sections of every sketch are actually functions themselves.

To simplify our use of functions, we will make sure that all the variables we use in the functions are declared in the beginning of the sketch. This way, we can pass data back and forth between the main sketch and each function.

When a variable is defined in the main part of the sketch, it can be used in any function. We call these variables ***global***. When the variable is declared inside the function, we call it ***local***. It can only be used inside the function. Its value goes away as soon as the code execution leaves the function.

Generally, once we start to use functions and get comfortable with them, we can literally write most of our sketch as functions and then just call functions in the void loop() part of the sketch. This makes for very clean, easy to organize and efficient code.

All we have to do is comment or uncomment the call statements for the function to turn it off or on.

Every function has a name. To help remind me that a key word is a function, I like to add to the beginning of the function's name, the letters, func_. For example, the two obvious names for the scope and strip chart are:

func_Scope()

func_StripChart()

To call the function, all we have to do is write its name in one line of the sketch. This shouts out to the sketch to grab the execution of the code contained in the function's definition. It's sort of like a spell in the Harry Potter books. Shout out its name and the spell is executed.

There are two parts to every function. First is the definition. This is done as a special section of code that begins with void.

There are two operations we've introduced so far we might want to re-write as functions:

- ✓ *Taking and displaying data like a scope*
- ✓ *Taking and displaying data like a stripchart recorder.*

Think about how you would organize your functions for these operations.

4.9 Final sketch for scope and strip chart recorder operation

Here is my sketch, cleaned up, that will either record data from the ADC at the fastest rate possible and display the results in either the scope mode or the strip chart recorder mode:

```
#include <avdwcb_AnalogReadFast.h>
```

```
//general measurements:
int pinADC = A1; // analog pin to read
float mV_per_ADU = 3300.0 / 660.25;
float V_ADU;
float V_mV;
float Time_point_sec;
// is the value of the time for each single point

//scope:
int npts_ave = 1; // pts to average in scope
const long npts_arr = 501;
int arrV_ADU[npts_arr];
float Time_X_usec;
float Time_point_msec;

//stripchart recorder:
long iTime_ave_usec = 1000;// if no tusing nPLC
int nPLC = 6; // does 0.1 sec averages
long iTime_stop_usec;
long iCounter1;
long iTime_start_usec;


//temp sensor:
float Temp_degC;
float Temp_degF;
int pinGND = A0;
int pin5V = A2;


void setup() {
  Serial.begin(2000000);
  pinMode (pinGND, OUTPUT);
  pinMode (pin5V, OUTPUT);
  digitalWrite (pinGND, LOW);
  digitalWrite (pin5V, HIGH);
  analogWrite(9, 200);
  if (nPLC != 0) {
    iTime_ave_usec = (nPLC / 60.0) * 1.0e6;
  }
}
void loop() {
  // decide which type of measurement with comments
  //func_StripChart();
  func_Scope();
}

//all the functions are placed after the void loop() section
void func_StripChart() {
  //initialize sums and counters
  V_ADU = 0.0;
```

```
  iCounter1 = 0;
  //calculate when to finish averaging
  iTime_stop_usec = micros() + iTime_ave_usec;
  while (micros() < iTime_stop_usec) {
    V_ADU = V_ADU + analogReadFast(pinADC);
    iCounter1++;
  }
  V_ADU = V_ADU / iCounter1;
  // we've got the averaged voltage value

  V_mV = V_ADU * mV_per_ADU;
  Time_point_sec = ((micros() - 0.5 * iTime_ave_usec)) * 1.0e-6;
  Temp_degC = V_mV / 10.0 - 50.0;
  Temp_degF = Temp_degC * 9 / 5 + 32;

  // decide what to print out with comments
  Serial.print(iCounter1); Serial.print(", ");
  Serial.print(Time_point_sec, 3); Serial.print(", ");
  //Serial.print(100); Serial.print(", ");
  Serial.print(V_ADU, 3); Serial.print(", ");
  Serial.println(V_mV, 3);
  //Serial.println(Temp_degC);
  //Serial.println(Temp_degF);
}

void func_Scope() {
  //initialize the array for the running sum
  for (int j = 1; j < npts_arr; j++) {
    arrV_ADU[j] = 0.0;
  }

  iTime_start_usec = micros();
  for (int j = 1; j < npts_arr; j++) {
    for (int i = 1; i <= npts_ave; i++) {
      arrV_ADU[j] = arrV_ADU[j] + analogReadFast(pinADC);
    }
    // finished averaging for each array element

  }
  // finished filling entire array
  Time_X_usec = (micros() - iTime_start_usec * 1.0);
  Time_X_usec = Time_X_usec / (npts_arr - 1);

  // now printing the array values
  for (int j = 1; j < npts_arr; j++) {
    V_ADU = arrV_ADU[j] / (npts_ave*1.0);
    V_mV = V_ADU * mV_per_ADU;
    Temp_degC = V_mV / 10.0 - 50.0;
    Temp_degF = Temp_degC * 9 / 5 + 32;
    Time_point_msec = j * Time_X_usec * 1.0e-3;

    // decide what to print out
    Serial.print(j); Serial.print(", ");
    Serial.print(Time_X_usec); Serial.print(", ");
    //Serial.print(Time_point_msec, 3); Serial.print(", ");
    //Serial.print(100); Serial.print(", ");
```

```
      Serial.print(V_ADU, 3); Serial.print(", ");
      Serial.println(V_mV, 3);
      //Serial.println(Temp_degC);
      //Serial.println(Temp_degF);
    }
    delay(10000); // wait for view screen
}
```

4.10 When to plot as a scope and when to plot as a strip chart recorder?

On the serial plotter, we can only plot 500 points at any time. If each point is 10 msec, the horizontal scale would be 500 points x 0.01 sec = 5 sec full scale.

To average for 10 msec using the scope function would require about 10 msec/(16 usec/pt) = 600 points averaged.

This is about my limit of patience. I don't want to wait more than 5 second until I see the data displayed.

If I take data with an averaging time of less than 10 msec per point, then I will display the data as a scope and use an array to record the data and display it, one full screen at a time.

But, if I am using more than 10 msec averaging, I will increase it to 1 PLC, 16.67 msec per averaged point and take the averaged points and display them right away, so the display looks more like a strip chart recorder.

In this case, the time base for a full screen of data is 500 points x 16.7 msec/point = 8.5 seconds. A setting of 2 PLCs is a fullscale screen of 17 sec. And, a setting of 3 PLCs, 50 msec/point, is 25 sec full scale.

This is not a hard and fast rule, but a guide I use to determine the sketch I run and the type of display I end up with. This is just a personal preference and depends somewhat on what I am looking for.

4.11 Revisiting the TMP36 in stripchart mode

The temperature sensor varies slowly. Using an averaging time of 6 power line cycles is 0.1 second, or 500 points x 0.1 sec/point = 50 sec full scale on the serial plotter. This is an ideal average for the temperature sensor. The sensitivity will not change but the noise will be improved a little bit.

Figure 4.8 shows the measured response of the temperature sensor using an averaging of 6 PLCs, after it was touched. This is as good as can be done with the 10-bit ADC.

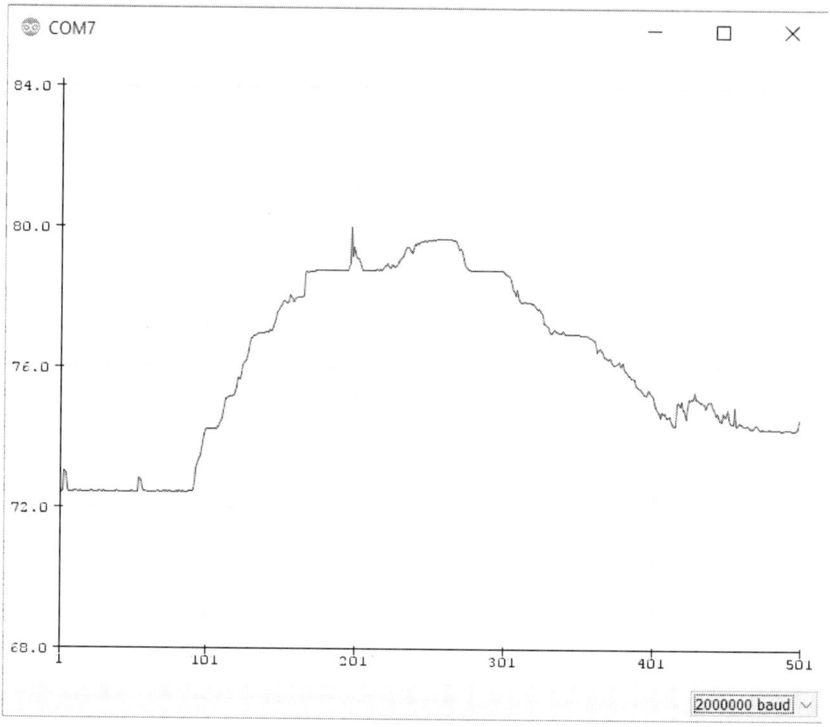

Figure 4.8. Measured temperature on the TMP36 sensor using strip chart recorder mode, nPLC=6, after touching.

With nPLC = 6, there is 100 msec per point. With 500 points full scale, this is 50 seconds full scale. The temperature steps from the 5 mV / level resolution of the 10-bit ADC are still present, but the averaging does reduce the noise a little bit. We cannot do any better unless we use a higher bit resolution, which we cover in the next section.

4.12 Increasing the temperature resolution using a 16-bit ADC

We see a fundamental limitation with this ADC. The smallest change we can see is only 5 mV. This corresponds to 0.5 degC. It sure would be nice if we could measure smaller changes in temperature than 0.5 degC.

Unfortunately, this means we have to measure a smaller voltage than 5 mV. We can't do this with the built in ADC in the Atmega328, the brains of the Arduino Uno board.

But we can do it using an external 16-bit ADC. In a following chapter we will see how to do this using a very low cost 16-bit ADC.

At 16-bit resolution, there are 2^{16} -1 levels. This is about 65,500 levels. If we use a scale of 2 V full scale at 16-bit resolution, each level corresponds to a voltage level of 2 V/65,500 = 31 uV = 0.031 mV per level.

With a temperature sensitivity of 1 degC/10 mV and a sensitivity level of 0.031 mV, the temperature sensitivity is 1 degC/10 mV x 0.031 mV = 0.003 degC. This is 3 milli degC per level, a very sensitive scale.

Before we switch to a 16-bit ADC, though, we can explore how else we can capture the measurements to store or display.

Chapter 5. All the Ways of Saving or Displaying the Measurements

Acquiring the actual measurements is only the starting place. They don't mean anything unless we do something with the information. The most basic operation is to display and store the data.

We've seen the basic steps in displaying the data either on the serial printer or the serial plotter. Now that we have these basic steps, we can explore adding some valuable features.

5.1 General data acquisition modes

So far, we have established a simple measurement process that allows us to take averaged measurements with two modes of operation:

Scope mode with 1 to 100 consecutive averages for 16 usec or 1.6 msec per point or 8 msec to 0.8 sec full scale.

Strip chart recorder mode for 1 to 60 PLC or a time of 17 msec to 1 second per point.

We've shown how we can plot the data like on a scope or strip chart recorder on the serial plotter. If we print the measurements to the serial printer, we can always copy the data from the screen and paste into excel. But we can do more with the data to make the analysis much easier.

5.2 Datalogging data directly into a text file using a terminal emulator

So far, we looked at three ways of getting data from the Arduino:

1. *printing directly on the Serial Monitor*
2. *plotting directly on the Serial Plotter*
3. *copying data from the Serial Monitor and pasting it into a spreadsheet*

In each case, the data was sent over the serial com link to the computer. The Arduino IDE has a built-in function which reads the data on the serial com link and does something with it.

The built in Serial Monitor is an example of a general tool called a *terminal emulator*. This is named for the "dumb" terminals consisting of a cathode ray tube (CRT) monitor and keyboard we used to use to communicate with computers in the "olden days."

When we emulate a simple terminal which just reads and writes data to and from the serial com link, we call it a *terminal* or *terminal emulator*.

The Serial Monitor is a very simple version of a terminal emulator. Once you set its baud rate to receive data to the same rate at which the Arduino is set to transmit using the Serial.begin() command, the Serial Monitor displays the characters transmitted on the serial com link.

It has a buffer to store the data as it comes in so we can scroll up and down the transmitted data.

As in most tools, there is a balance between feature richness and ease of use. In the case of the Serial Monitor, it is really easy to use, but doesn't really have many features.

However, there are other terminal emulator programs for any operating system which have more features.

Sparkfun offers a great review of terminal program options for all operating systems.

Of all the terminal emulators for windows, my favorite is *Yet Another Terminal* (YAT). You can Download it from this wiki page.

You will need to scroll to the bottom of this page and click on the large green "*download*" button. Once the .exe file downloads, click on the .exe program to install it. Use all the default conditions.

Run the YAT program. When the program opens, you will see a simple screen, as shown in Figure 5.1. Before we can use it to read the data coming down the serial port, we have to adjust a few settings.

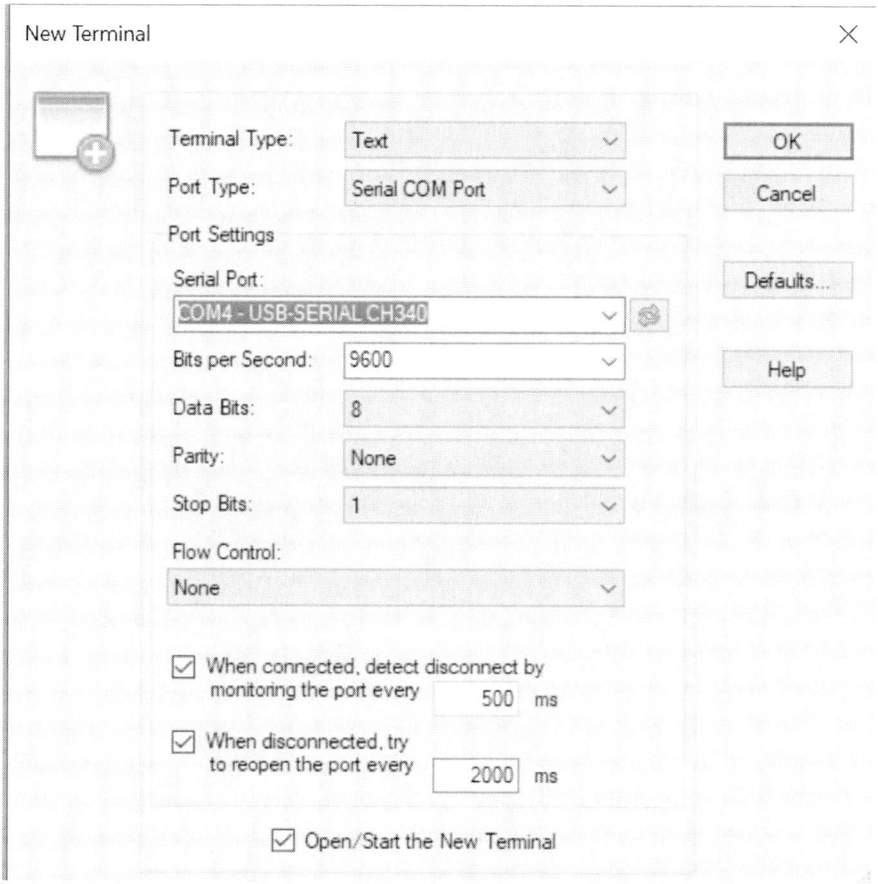

Figure 5.1 The opening screen for YAT.

If this page does not open, under the Terminal menu, scroll to the bottom and select the settings option, as shown in Figure 5.2.

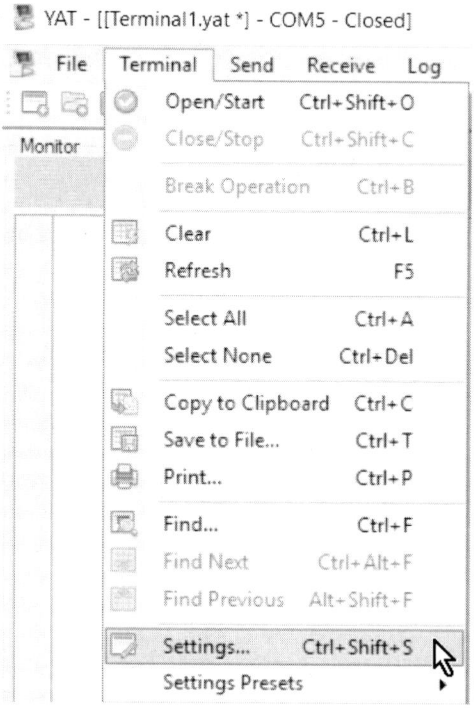

Figure 5.2 Select the Settings option in the Terminal menu.

When this screen opens up there are really only a few settings to adjust. The settings window is shown in Figure 5.3. Make sure your settings are set to these default values.

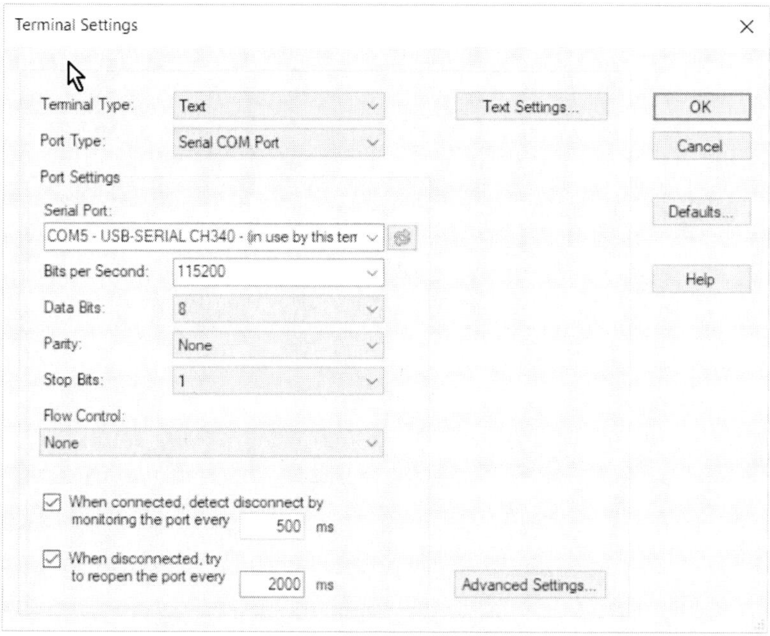

Figure 5.3. Select the com port and the baud rate to match the Arduino.

The two most important settings are the port connection and the baud rate. Take a look at the baud rate options. There is no 2,000,000 option.

These are the same two settings we had to adjust before we could use the Serial Monitor tool.

You can experiment with the highest baud rate you can send and receive reliable data just as we did in the *Saturday Afternoon Low-Cost Electronics Projects* series, Arduinos Without Tears.

I found 115200 baud as the fastest, available speed that always worked.

Once these two settings are adjusted, and the baud rate in the sketch matches the baud rate in YAT, the terminal is ready to read the serial monitor.

Only one device can use the serial link at any time. When we upload a sketch to the Arduino, we are using the serial com link. To upload the sketch over the serial link, you first have to stop the terminal emulator. This is found under the Terminal menu. Select the start or stop command to stop the terminal monitor to upload the sketch, then turn on the monitor to display the data coming over the serial link from the Arduino.

We can use the most recent sketch in the previous section to print data to the serial monitor. After we run this sketch, data is coming over the serial com link. We just need to turn YAT on to display this data.

Under the Terminal menu, select Start, as shown in Figure 5.4. When the terminal starts received data is displayed on the main window. This is where all the magic can happen.

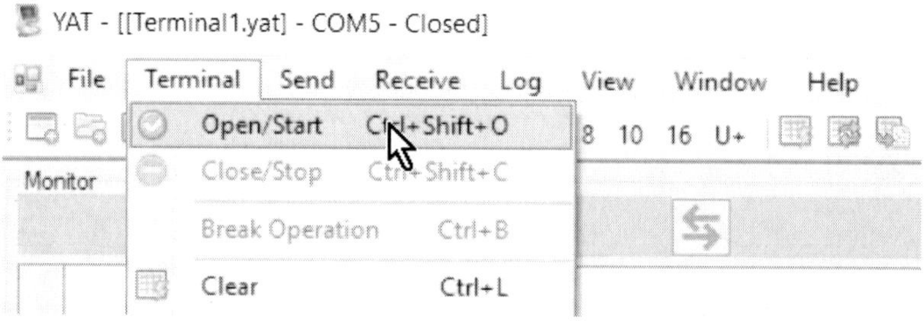

Figure 5.4. To have YAT display the data coming in over the serial monitor just click start, under the terminal menu.

In its simplest form, YAT will act just like the Serial Monitor. It will display the characters that come in over the serial com link, like as shown in Figure 5.5.

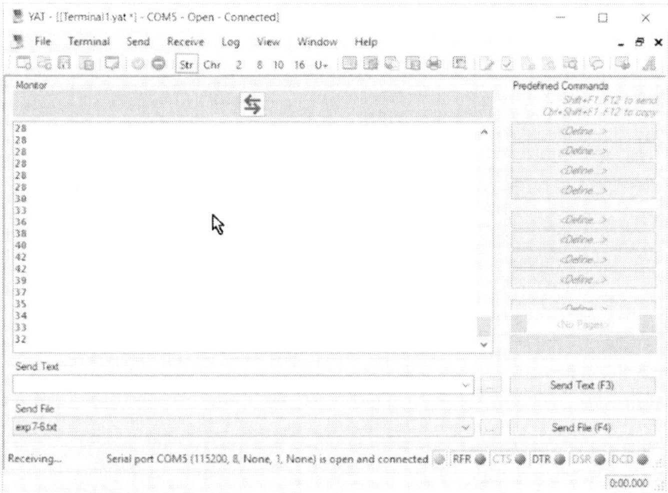

Figure 5.5 An example of the data read on YAT as it comes in from the Arduino just like on the Serial Monitor.

5.3 Experiment: data logging measurements with a date stamp

In addition to the data coming in from the Arduino, we can also add a date stamp, a time stamp and a delta time since the terminal opened, stamp. All of this information is added to the data by the computer. There are no changes we require in the sketch.

To activate these features, we pull down the View menu and select *Show Time Stamp* and *Show Time Span*, as shown in Figure 5.6.

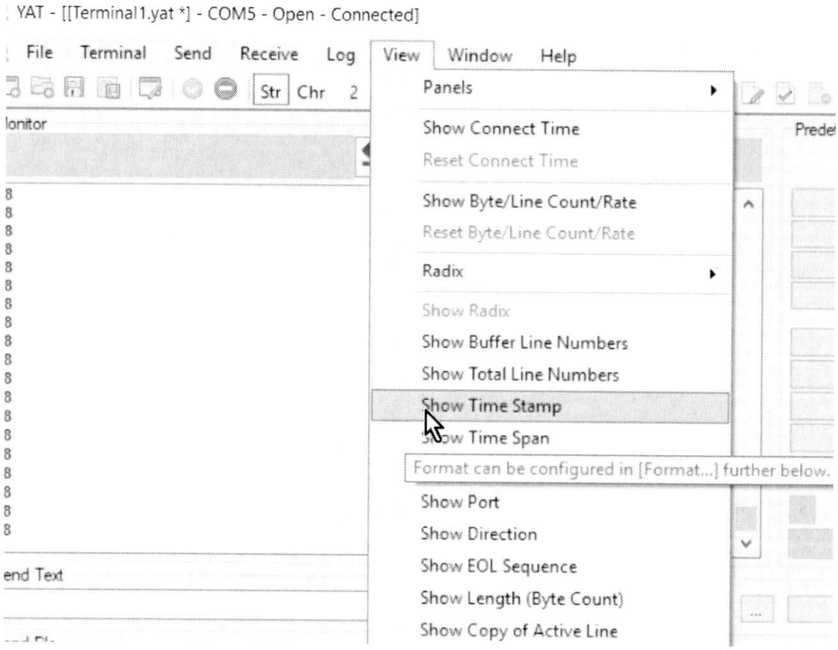

Figure 5.6. Under the View menu, select the Show time Stamp and Show Time Delta.

In addition, we can format the display of this information under the format item at the bottom of the View menu. The format screen allows us to create a convenient style for the data in the window. My own personal preference uses three important features:

1. *Use a **different color** for each type of data. This makes it easy to tell what is what in each column.*

2. *Use a **comma AND space** to separate the data on the monitor. This will help when exporting the data into a file.*

3. ***No enclosure**. This will print just the numbers, without brackets {} or parentheses ().*

My selections are shown in Figure 5.7.

Figure 5.7 Set the format for displaying the time stamp, time range and delimiters.

Using these settings, we can display the measured data from the Arduino with the date and time for each point and the time span from the time the terminal window was opened up.

All this data is added to the data coming over from the Arduino, based on the real time clock in the PC recording the serial com link. The final screen is shown in Figure 5.8. This is the data we want to save and later import into a spreadsheet.

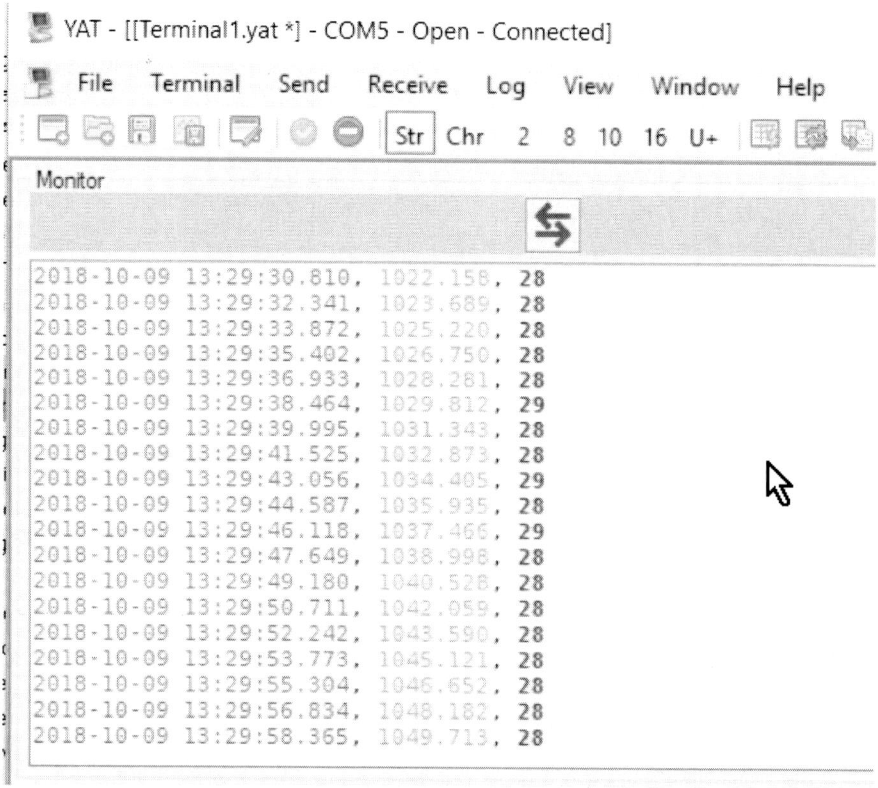

Figure 5.8 Final data recorded on the screen with the time stamp information and the Arduino data.

5.4 Experiment: Importing data from a text file directly into a spreadsheet

We've already seen how we can plot data directly as it comes from the Arduino using the Serial Plotter tool built into the Arduino IDE.

We've also seen that we can literally copy the data from the Serial Monitor and paste it into any spreadsheet. We can do the same from the YAT screen.

In addition, there is another way of getting data directly into a spreadsheet: save it to a file and import the file.

One of the cool features of YAT is to log the data that comes in over the serial link along with the time stamp information, directly into a text file. This file can be opened by any spreadsheet tool.

We can set YAT up to write each line of data that comes in on the serial com link into a file and save it as it comes in. This can be a text file and replicate exactly what you see on the screen.

This way we can save long records of data and not lose any of it and have it available for immediate import.

To set up YAT to data log the file, we open up the log menu item and select settings at the bottom of the list. This is shown in Figure 5.9.

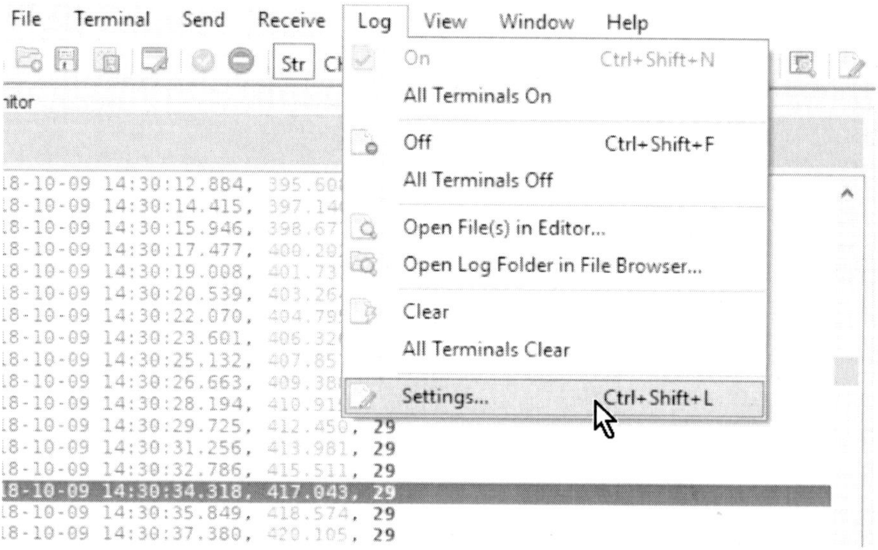

Figure 5.9 To set up a file for data logging, pull down the Log menu item and select the settings item at the bottom.

In this settings window, the most important settings, as shown in Figure 5.10, are:

1. *The directory to store the log file.*
2. *Use Neat outputs so that all the time stamp information is included*
3. *Log received data*
4. *If you select Append if file exists, every time you close the terminal and open it, the data will be written to the same file. I usually use this feature.*
5. *If you select the Create separate files button, every time you stop the terminal and start it up, a new file will be created.*

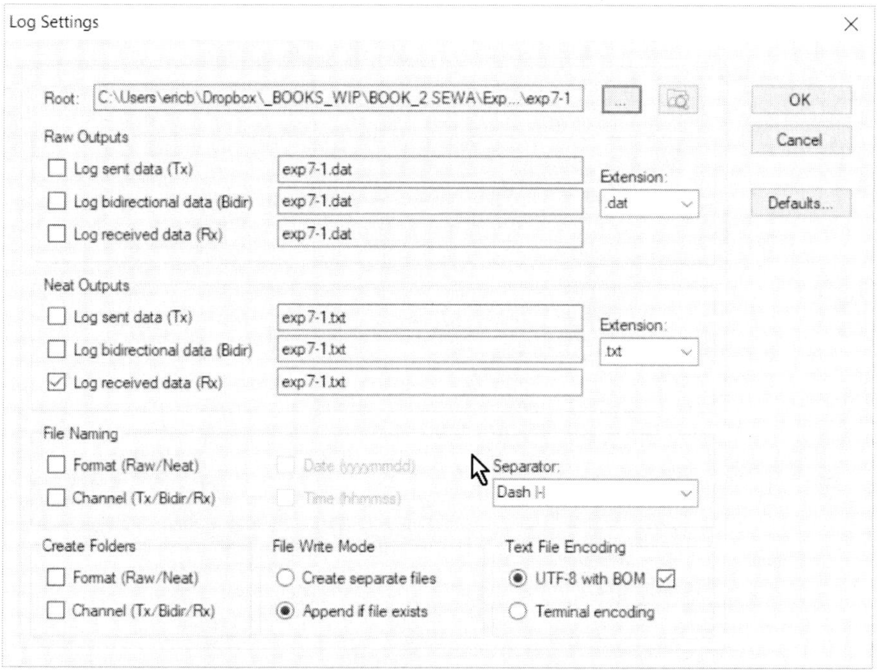

Figure 5.10 We want to find a directly to place the log file and use the settings as marked.

Once the log setup is complete, it's a simple matter of selecting log on from the log menu and instantly, you are creating a file with the serial data and its date stamp information.

Figure 5.11 is an example of the data in the text file. The first column is the date, then the time and then the elapsed time since the terminal window was opened and finally, the measured data.

exp7-12.txt - Notepad

File Edit Format View Help

```
2018-10-09 14:53:39.810, 013.727, 29
2018-10-09 14:53:41.340, 015.257, 29
2018-10-09 14:53:42.871, 016.788, 29
2018-10-09 14:53:44.403, 018.320, 29
2018-10-09 14:53:45.934, 019.851, 29
2018-10-09 14:53:47.465, 021.382, 29
2018-10-09 14:53:48.995, 022.912, 29
2018-10-09 14:53:50.525, 024.442, 29
2018-10-09 14:53:52.057, 025.974, 29
2018-10-09 14:53:53.588, 027.505, 29
2018-10-09 14:53:55.118, 029.035, 29
2018-10-09 14:53:56.650, 030.567, 29
2018-10-09 14:53:58.181, 032.098, 29
2018-10-09 14:53:59.712, 033.629, 29
2018-10-09 14:54:01.242, 035.159, 29
2018-10-09 14:54:02.773, 036.690, 29
2018-10-09 14:54:04.304, 038.221, 29
2018-10-09 14:54:05.835, 039.752, 29
2018-10-09 14:54:07.365, 041.282, 29
```

Figure 5.11. An example of the data stored in the text file using the YAT logging feature.

This data is automatically saved and ready for import into a spreadsheet.

We can open this text file with a spreadsheet tool, like Excel and separate each column of data into a separate column in the spreadsheet. The only secret is to use the delimit option to convert the text file into columns of meaningful data. An example of doing this is shown in Figure 5.12.

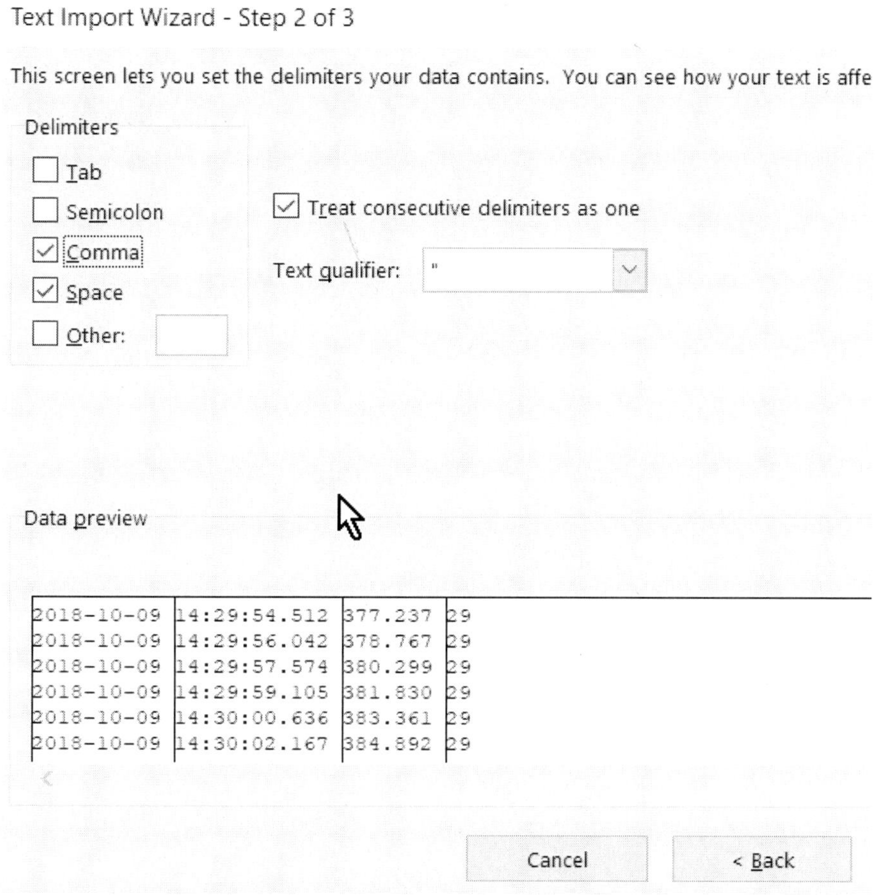

Figure 5.12. When opening a txt file in excel you are given the option how to interpret the columns. Select delimit and comma and space for perfect importing.

Once in excel, we can turn on the power of spreadsheet analysis and plotting.

5.5 Data Logging Directly into an Excel Spreadsheet

In the last experiment, we recorded the time and date stamp and the other data and wrote all this data into a text file using a free terminal emulation software tool. We could then open the file using any spreadsheet and use the plotting features of a spreadsheet to plot the data.

If you have a PC and run Microsoft Excel, you can record the information that comes over the serial port directly, write it into the columns of an excel spreadsheet and plot the data as it comes in.

To accomplish this, we will use a free software tool called PLX-DAX v2.

5.6 New Tool: PLX-DAQ v2

In this section, I will introduce you to PLX-DAQ v2, which is a simple to use macro written inside MS excel to automatically read the serial port and move the readings directly into the spreadsheet.

The original version of PLX-DAQ was written for the PIC microcontroller. It worked in some cases for the Arduino but was limited in functionality.

This tool was re-written from scratch and dramatically improved by Jonathan Arndt, who goes by the handle Net^Devil.

The latest version of this tool can be downloaded from here. As of this writing, the latest version is version v2.11. Always download the latest version.

The software is basically an excel spreadsheet with an embedded macro. Unfortunately, it only runs on a windows version of excel since it heavily uses the macros built into excel.

All it really does is read (or write) data on the serial com port, sent over to it from your Arduino sketch. The macro reads this data and carries out the commands based on key words it reads. Simple commands are built into the macro.

From the Arduino, we just print a few keywords to the com port, which are read and understood by this macro. The macro in excel reads the serial port and follows the commands it receives.

To write data directly into the excel spreadsheet, we run the code in the sketch. Then we open up an excel file that has this macro running.

This free software tool will enable us to take information from the Arduino, like measured data, write it into an excel spreadsheet, plot it as we go, and save the worksheet, all automatically.

The way we do this is by adding the directions to excel as code words in an Arduino sketch. These code words will direct excel to do things for us automatically like printing labels to columns, printing data into specific columns and even saving the worksheet.

In this first simple experiment, we will take advantage of just six

key-word commands we will embed in an Arduino sketch:

CLEARSHEET: when this keyword is printed on the serial com link by the Arduino code, the excel macro will read it and clear all the data on the active worksheet, including the labels. If you are starting a new experiment and want to initialize the spreadsheet for new data, this should be the first command sent over the serial link.

The command in the Arduino sketch would be

```
Serial.println("CLEARSHEET");
```

CLEARDATA: this command, when received by the excel macro from the serial link, will clear only the data in the spreadsheet starting at row 2 and moving down the spreadsheet. It will retain the labels which are printed in row 1.

The command in the Arduino sketch would be:

Serial.println("CLEARDATA");

CLEARRANGE(A,1,C,300): this command will clear the cells identified from the upper left cell, A1, to the lower right cell, C300, specified. I like using this command when I have formulas already set up in other columns that I do not want cleared out each time I start a new run and want to remove old data.

LABEL: this command will write the titles for the columns in the excel spreadsheet. Its format is

Serial.println("LABEL, 1st column, 2nd column, 3rd column, last column");

DATA: this is the fundamental command to write some information into the next row of the spreadsheet. The information after the DATA command will parsed data values into each adjacent next column with each data item separated by a comma.

The command in the Arduino sketch to print two variables into two different columns would be:

```
Serial.println("DATA,");
Serial.print(var1);Serial.print(",  ");
Serial.println(var2);
```

SAVEWORKBOOK: when this keyword is sent to the serial port, the macro will save the current worksheet using the file name it had when you opened it.

These key words are added to a sketch and placed in Serial.print statements so they are printed to the serial com.

The excel spreadsheet will listen to the com port and read these key words. The macro will perform internal operations based on the key words it reads.

In the spreadsheet, we will insert an excel graph so we can not only save the data to the excel file, but also plot it as it comes in.

5.7 Recording and plotting data directly in excel

In this first example, we will only set up excel to record some dummy data and plot it as we go.

The most common application for PLX-DAQ is to data log data at specific time intervals. In this sort of application, the exact date and time each data point was recorded might be important. In this case, we can take advantage of three built in key words used by the macro to track time.

In addition to writing variables into each cell in the excel spreadsheet, we can use special key words which the macro will translate into specific values or actions.

There are three specific key words we will use to tell the macro to print time information. They are:

The keyword ***DATE*** is read by the macro and printed in the cell as the current date.

The keyword ***TIME*** is read by the macro and printed in the cell as the current time.

The keyword ***TIMER*** is read by the macro and printed in the cell as seconds since the start of pressing the connect button.

In this example, we will set up five columns in excel. They will be:

1. *Current date (we will use the **DATE** key word)*

2. *Current time (we will use the **TIME** key word)*
3. *Elapsed time in seconds (we will use the **TIMER** key word)*
4. *The number of points we have exported*
5. *A random number from 0 to 9*

The first step is to clear out the spreadsheet and start from scratch. The CLEARSHEET command will erase all the columns but WILL NOT erase the plots we have on the spreadsheet, just the data.

This way, if we have a plot template we like, we just keep it and can still clear the spreadsheet.

The second step is to print the labels of each column in the first row.

The last step is to start printing the data into each column.

The code to clear the sheet and write the labels will only happen once, so it should be placed in the void setup() function. It would look like this:

```
void setup() {
  Serial.begin(2000000);
  Serial.println("CLEARSHEET"); // clears sheet
  Serial.println("LABEL, Date, Time, Timer, Count, Random");
}
```

Notice that we are sending data over the serial port at 2000000 baud. This data rate must match the data rate in the PLX-DAQ control panel. Any data rate will work as long as they match between the sketch and the excel spreadsheet PLX-DAQ control panel. I routinely use 2000000 with no problems.

However, the excel interface is only stable at slow data transfer rates. We will have to slow down the rate we send data to excel so it can keep up with collecting the data and adding it to the spreadsheet. Otherwise it will crash.

When the excel spreadsheet opens up, we will see the control panel for the macros, as displayed in Figure 5.13.

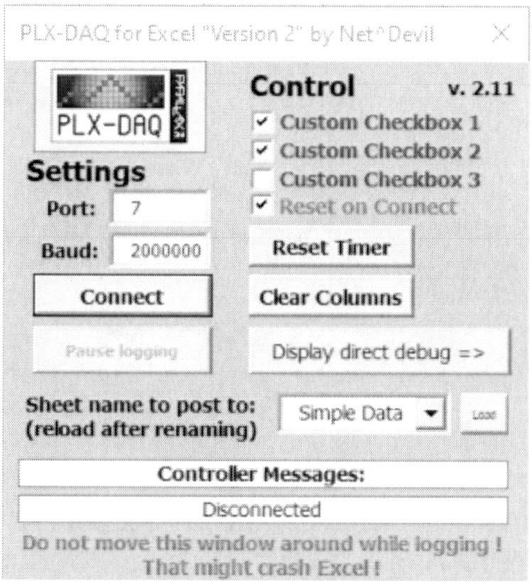

Figure 5.13. The control panel for the macro, displayed in the open excel workbook. Note that the baud rate and com port must match the same as the baud rate set up in the sketch and the com port for the Arduino.

The complete sketch to calculate the random number and print out the data is the following:

```
// simple test of the PLX-DAQ
int i = 0;
void setup() {
  Serial.begin(2000000);
  Serial.println("CLEARSHEET"); // clears sheet
  Serial.println("LABEL, Date, Time, Timer, Count, Random");
}
void loop() {
  Serial.print("DATA, DATE, TIME, TIMER,");
  Serial.print(i++); Serial.print(",");
  Serial.println(random(0, 10));
```

```
  delay(200); // delay sending data to keep excel from crashing
}
```

We need to add one line in the beginning of the sketch to declare the variable, i, as an integer. We use this to count the number of iterations.

The first line in the `void loop` () function will print the first three columns of information to the macros. The key word DATA in the beginning will be read by the macro as a command. It will consider all the following terms as information to be placed in the spreadsheet cells.

The following three keywords, DATE, TIME, TIMER will be read by the macro which will tell it to print the current date, time and time in seconds since the start of the connect, to be printed in the consecutive cells on the same row.

The next two lines will print specific numbers in the next cells on the same row. It's not until the last command, Serial.println() is received that the last data will be placed at the end of the row and then the line feed command in the `Serial.println`() line will start printing the data on the next row of the excel spreadsheet.

I added a delay(200); as the last line just so that the data will come into the excel spreadsheet slow enough for excel to read it. There are some limits to how fast we can print data into the macro. We will explore these limits in a follow-on experiment.

Once this sketch has been uploaded to the Arduino, it will immediately start running in the Atmega 328 microcontroller on the Arduino board. It will generate the numbers and print the text to the serial com link, whether or not any device is listening on the computer end.

To actually have this data come into excel, we have to run the macro in excel by pressing the "Connect" button in the PLX-DAQ control box. This will tell the excel macro to start reading the data on the serial com link.

In the PLX-DAQ control panel, the fourth line down under the word "control", written in red, will enable or not enable a reset on connect command to be sent to the Arduino when you Connect, or turn on the macro. When this box is checked, the macro will send a reset command to the Arduino which will cause it to start the sketch over again. This is a good thing to do.

When we press the Connect button, the macro will send the reset command to the Arduino. This will force the Arduino to start the sketch from the beginning. The spreadsheet will be cleared, the labels will be printed, and data will be written to the serial com link and immediately read by the macro and printed into the spreadsheet.

An example of the spreadsheet with some data, is shown in Figure 5.14.

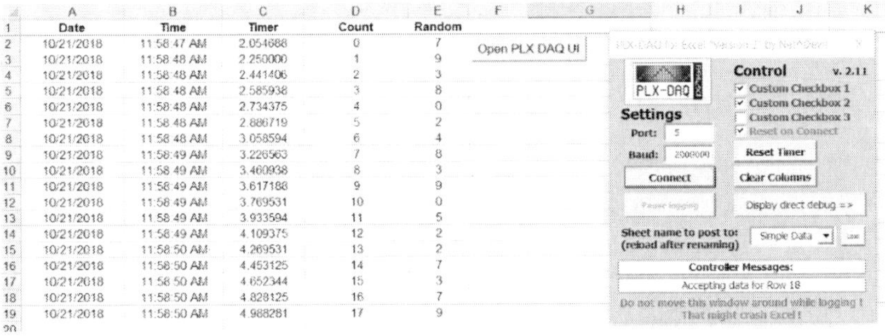

	A	B	C	D	E
1	Date	Time	Timer	Count	Random
2	10/21/2018	11:58:47 AM	2.054688	0	7
3	10/21/2018	11:58:48 AM	2.250000	1	9
4	10/21/2018	11:58:48 AM	2.441406	2	3
5	10/21/2018	11:58:48 AM	2.585938	3	8
6	10/21/2018	11:58:48 AM	2.734375	4	0
7	10/21/2018	11:58:48 AM	2.886719	5	2
8	10/21/2018	11:58:48 AM	3.058594	6	4
9	10/21/2018	11:58:49 AM	3.226563	7	8
10	10/21/2018	11:58:49 AM	3.460938	8	3
11	10/21/2018	11:58:49 AM	3.617188	9	9
12	10/21/2018	11:58:49 AM	3.769531	10	0
13	10/21/2018	11:58:49 AM	3.933594	11	5
14	10/21/2018	11:58:49 AM	4.109375	12	2
15	10/21/2018	11:58:50 AM	4.269531	13	2
16	10/21/2018	11:58:50 AM	4.453125	14	7
17	10/21/2018	11:58:50 AM	4.652344	15	3
18	10/21/2018	11:58:50 AM	4.828125	16	7
19	10/21/2018	11:58:50 AM	4.988281	17	9

Figure 5.14. An example of the data as displayed in excel for this simple sketch.

Since the data is now in an excel spreadsheet, we can take advantage of the power of excel and plot the data as it comes in.

With a little sample data already present, we select the columns we want to plot like D and E, and then insert a graph. For this example, I like an x-y scatter plot. We will plot the data in column D, the counter, as the x, horizontal axis, and the random values, in column E, as the Y or vertical values.

When the graph icon is inserted, the data already in columns D and E will be plotted. If the entire columns were selected, then both axes will be auto scaled by default. As new data comes in with higher count values, the graph will automatically adjust to fit and plot this new data.

Figure 5.15 shows an example with a simple plot inserted and data plotted as it comes in.

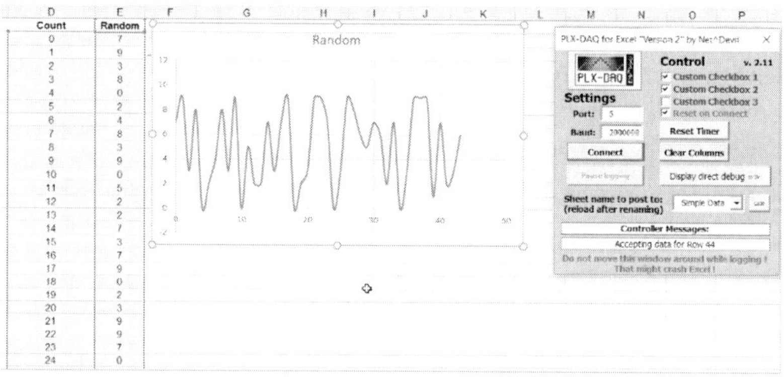

Figure 5.15. An example of the simple plot of the data in the excel spreadsheet as it comes in.

5.8 Two problems to avoid

There are two important problems to watch out for.

Problem #1: When the rate at which data comes into excel is faster than it can be plotted, you will lose some data and excel may crash.

Plotting each data point as it comes in takes some computing overhead by excel. The more points that are plotted and the graph refreshed, the longer it takes to add a new point. This means when it is plotting the data, excel is not listening to the serial port and getting the data to plot.

There is a small buffer in the com port. When data is read from the com buffer, it is removed from the com buffer and room is made for new data. When the rate at which the buffer is filled by the Arduino sketch is faster than the rate at which the data is read and cleared by excel, the buffer can overload, and you lose some data. In this case excel becomes unstable and it will crash.

In this simple sketch, we adjust the rate at which data is written to the serial port using the delay() function. As long as there are less than about 500 points to plot, a 200 msec delay between printing points to the com port is stable.

The fastest rate excel can read the data and plot it as it comes depends on how much data is already present in the spreadsheet (the re-plotting overhead it has to do in the background) and how often the data is printed to the serial port.

If you turn off auto calculate on the Formulas ribbon, you can send data to excel faster. But then, you lose the benefit of seeing it plotted as it comes in.

When sending random data over the com port, a delay function can control the rate of data transfer. If there will only be 100 points recorded, a print time between points of as short at 100 msec maybe stable.

A delay of 100 msec can sometimes send data over the com port too fast for excel to keep up. Pretty soon, we get a gap in the received data. This appears in the graph, as shown in Figure 5.16.

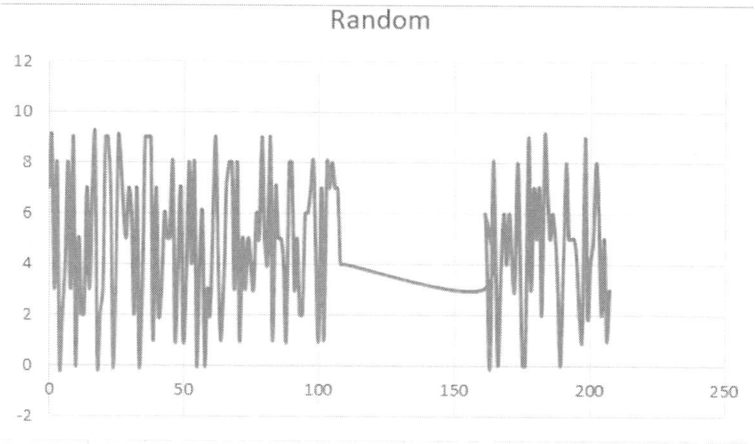

Figure 5.16. An example of printing data with a 100 msec delay showing a gap in receiving data when the plotting takes too much time and we are losing data.

To avoid this problem, we want to send data over the com port at a slow enough rate. If there will be 100-500 points, a delay of 0.15 sec is required. If there will be 500-1000 points, a delay of 0.2 sec may be needed. For more than 1000 points, a delay of 0.5 seconds is needed. Even then, excel will become unstable with more than 2500 points being replotted.

Try this experiment: Starting with a delay of 200 msec, decrease the delay time and let at least 200 points come in. What is the shortest delay that will give stable readings?

Problem #2: In order to upload code to the Arduino when we load a new sketch, the com port cannot also be open by the excel macro.

This means to upload a new or modified sketch to the Arduino, we have to make sure the PLX-DAQ macro has been disconnected. The "connect" switch toggles back and forth between "connect" and “disconnect.” This alternatively ties up or releases the com port of the PC.

Luckily, this is a simple problem to avoid. If you get an error that upload to the Arduino failed, chances are, it is because the macro is still connected to the com port. Just press disconnect and try uploading to the Arduino again.

5.9 Automatically saving a workbook

The key word to have the macro execute a save command for the current workbook is ***SAVEWORKBOOK***. We want to be sure to save the current workbook periodically so that we don't lose much data in the event excel crashes.

We should choose an interval that is long enough to not take up a lot of overhead but short enough, so we don't lose too much data if the computer crashes.

Depending on the application and the rate at which we generate data, about every 1-10 minutes is a good saving interval.

We need to keep track of the current time when each data point is recorded. When the current time reaches the time we want to save the workbook we should execute a ***SAVEWORKBOOK*** command.

Try this experiment: How would you implement this routine?

The special command I added is an if statement. I created a new variable, iTime_LastSave_msec as the counter keeping track of when the last save happened, as measured in msec on the millis() timer.

If the current time is greater than the time we should save again, we execute the save command. This is done in the following code:

```
if (millis() > iTime_LastSave_msec + iTime_SaveInterval_min * 60000) {
      Serial.println("BEEP");
      Serial.println("SAVEWORKBOOK");
      iTime_LastSave_msec = millis();
}
```

When implementing this algorithm, there is one very important potential problem to pay attention to.

There are two ways of storing integer information, as an int and as a long. They differ by up to how high a whole number they can count. An int can count up to 32,768, while a long can count up to over 2,147,483,648.

When we create an integer as an int, all the arithmetic we do with the number will be calculated as int math. If in the calculation, the result is over 32,768, it will roll over and may appear as a negative number.

If we want to do any future calculations using integer math, which might result in a number greater than 32,768, we should be sure to declare all the integer variables as long. This will keep all the digits we need through all the calculation.

This is especially important for the iTime_SaveInterval_min variable. While this number will only be as much as 100, easily stored as an int, it is used in calculations which could result in numbers as high as 100,000. If we created this variable as an int, it would roll over when it is larger than 32,768 and return incorrect calculations.

This is why this variable is created as a long.

5.10 Complete Sketch: data logging directly into MS excel

The final sketch we've developed will measure data from the ADC in scope mode or strip chart mode and either average it or write it directly to the serial com port where we can:

- ✓ *View the data on the serial monitor*
- ✓ *View the data on the serial plotter*
- ✓ *Data log the data into a text file*
- ✓ *Send the data to excel and plot it in real time*

Here is the final sketch:

```
// www.HackingPhysics.com data acquisition
// Eric Bogatin

#include <avdweb_AnalogReadFast.h>
// for the fastest ADC access- why not?


//excel specific variables:
int iFlag_xcel = 1; //1 means print to excel, 0 means do not
long iTime_SaveInterval_min = 1; // how often to save strip chart
long iTime_LastSave_msec = 0;
int delay_xcel_msec = 150;// delay for the scope print out

//general measurements:
int pinADC = A2;
float mV_per_ADU = 3300.0 / 660.25;
float V_ADU;
float V_mV;
float Time_point_sec;
float Time_X_usec;
float Time_point_msec;
long index_val = 0;

//scope:
int npts_ave = 1;
const long npts_arr = 501;
int arrV_ADU[npts_arr];

//stripchart recorder:
long iTime_ave_usec = 1000;
long npts_run = 1000;
float V_0_ADU;
// select one of the following by commenting/uncommenting
//int nPLC = 0; //set to 0 for hard coded averaging
//int nPLC = 1; //17 msec/point
//int nPLC = 3; //50 msec/point
//int nPLC = 6; //100 msec/point
int nPLC = 12; //200 msec/point
//int nPLC = 30; //500 msec/point

long iTime_stop_usec;
```

```
long iCounter1;
long iTime_start_usec;//  stop watch

//temp sensor:
float Temp_degC;
float Temp_degF;
int pinGND = A0;
int pin5V = A2;


void setup() {
  Serial.begin(2000000);
  pinMode (pinGND, OUTPUT);
  pinMode (pin5V, OUTPUT);
  digitalWrite (pinGND, LOW);
  digitalWrite (pin5V, HIGH);
  analogWrite(9, 200);
  if (nPLC != 0) {
    iTime_ave_usec = (nPLC / 60.0) * 1.0e6;
  }
}

void loop() {
  func_StripChart();
  // func_Scope();
}

void func_StripChart() {
  //if we want to use excel, then set up the labels:
  if (iFlag_xcel == 1) {
    //Serial.println("CLEARSHEET"); // clears entire sheet
    // will clear only some cells so we can keep formulas on sheet
    Serial.println("CLEARRANGE,A,1,C,3001");
   // clears from cell A1 to cell C3001
    Serial.println("LABEL, index, Time(sec), mV");
  }

  //stabilize the ADC input voltage to start clean
  for (int i = 1; i < 25; i++) {
      analogReadFast(pinADC);
    }

  //ready to take real measurements
  //record strip chart for a total of npts_run and then stop
  for (index_val = 1; index_val <= npts_run; index_val++) {
    V_ADU = 0.0;
    iCounter1 = 0;
    iTime_stop_usec = micros() + iTime_ave_usec;

    // start averaging loop
    while (micros() < iTime_stop_usec) {
```

```
      V_0_ADU = analogReadFast(pinADC);
      V_ADU = V_ADU + V_0_ADU ;
      iCounter1++;
    }
    //done with averaging

    Time_point_sec = ((micros() - 0.5 * iTime_ave_usec)) * 1.0e-6;
    V_ADU = V_ADU / iCounter1;
    V_mV = V_ADU * mV_per_ADU;
    Time_point_msec = Time_point_sec * 1.0e3;
    Temp_degC = V_mV / 10.0 - 50.0;
    Temp_degF = Temp_degC * 9 / 5 + 32;

    // if we print to excel then use right format
    // select what to print out
    if (iFlag_xcel == 1) {
      // print to excel options:
      Serial.print("DATA,");
      Serial.print(index_val); Serial.print(", ");
      Serial.print(Time_point_sec, 5); Serial.print(", ");
      Serial.println(Temp_degF, 3);
      //Serial.println(V_mV, 3);

      //save worksheet routine
      if (millis() > iTime_LastSave_msec + iTime_SaveInterval_min * 60000) {
        Serial.println("BEEP");
        Serial.println("SAVEWORKBOOK");
        iTime_LastSave_msec = millis();
      }
      else {
        // not printing to excel. Select serial monitor options
        Serial.print(index_val); Serial.print(", ");
        Serial.print(iCounter1); Serial.print(", ");
        Serial.print(Time_point_sec, 3); Serial.print(", ");
        //Serial.print(100); Serial.print(", ");
        //Serial.print(V_ADU, 3); Serial.print(", ");
        //Serial.println(V_mV, 3);
        //Serial.println(Temp_degC);
        Serial.println(Temp_degF);
      }
    }
  }
  // done taking all the points for this run. Ready to save
  Serial.println("SAVEWORKBOOK");
  while (1 != 2) {  //sit in infinite loop and wait
    Serial.println("BEEP");
    delay(1000);
  }
}


void func_Scope() {
  if (iFlag_xcel == 1) {
    // if we print to excel, set it up
    //Serial.println("CLEARSHEET"); // clears sheet
    Serial.println("CLEARRANGE,A,1,C,3001");
```

```
    Serial.println("LABEL, index, Time(sec), mV");
  }

  // initialize array
  for (int j = 1; j < npts_arr; j++) {
    arrV_ADU[j] = 0.0;
  }

  //stabilize the ADC input voltage to start clean
  for (int i = 1; i < 25; i++) {
      analogReadFast(pinADC);
    }
  //ready to take real measurements

  //begin quickly filling int array with averaged points
  iTime_start_usec = micros();
  for (int j = 1; j < npts_arr; j++) {
    for (int i = 1; i <= npts_ave; i++) {
      V_ADU = analogReadFast(pinADC);
      arrV_ADU[j] = arrV_ADU[j] + V_ADU;
    }
  }
  Time_X_usec = (micros() - iTime_start_usec * 1.0);
  Time_X_usec = Time_X_usec / (npts_arr - 1);

// begin printing out formated array contents
  for (index_val = 1; index_val < npts_arr; index_val++) {
    V_ADU = arrV_ADU[index_val] / npts_ave; // calc average
    V_mV = V_ADU * mV_per_ADU;
    Temp_degC = V_mV / 10.0 - 50.0;
    Temp_degF = Temp_degC * 9 / 5 + 32;
    Time_point_msec = index_val * Time_X_usec * 1.0e-3;
    Time_point_sec = index_val * Time_X_usec * 1.0e-6;

    if (iFlag_xcel == 1) {
      // if printing to excel, format the data
      Serial.print("DATA,");
      Serial.print(index_val); Serial.print(", ");
      Serial.print(Time_point_sec, 5); Serial.print(", ");
      Serial.println(V_mV, 3);
      delay(delay_xcel_msec);
    }
    else {
      //if not printing to excel, format for serial monitor
      Serial.print(index_val); Serial.print(", ");
      Serial.print(Time_X_usec); Serial.print(", ");
      Serial.print(Time_point_msec, 3); Serial.print(", ");
      //Serial.print(100); Serial.print(", ");
      Serial.print(V_ADU, 3); Serial.print(", ");
      Serial.println(V_mV, 3);
      //Serial.println(Temp_degC);
      //Serial.println(Temp_degF);
```

```
        }
    }
    // done printing the array

    if (iFlag_xcel == 1) {
      Serial.println("SAVEWORKBOOK");
      while (1 != 2) {// stay in loop after printing data
        Serial.println("BEEP");
        delay(1000);
      }
    }
    delay(2000); // wait to view screen
}
```

As examples of the output when interfacing to excel, I used first the strip chart mode and plotted 500 points at 6 PLCs or every 0.1 seconds in a run. An example of the excel spreadsheet measuring the temperature of a TMP36 sensor is shown in Figure 5.17. Note, I touched the sensor at about 10 second or 100 points into the run.

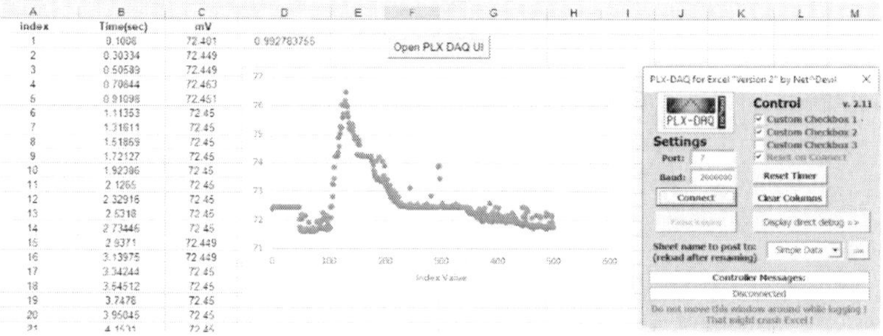

Figure 5.17. An example of the strip chart recorder output, 50 seconds full scale. Note, the resolution of the ADC is only 0.5 degrees C or about 0.9 degF.

Using the scope mode of operation, I set the npts_ave = 1 so the data came out as fast as possible roughly every 30 usec. At 500 points, this is about 15 msec of total data. Figure 5.18 shows the excel graph of this 15 msec measurement period. Note the temperature resolution of the ADC, at 5 mV and 1 degC/10 mV or 0.9 degF resolution, which is the transition observed on the plot.

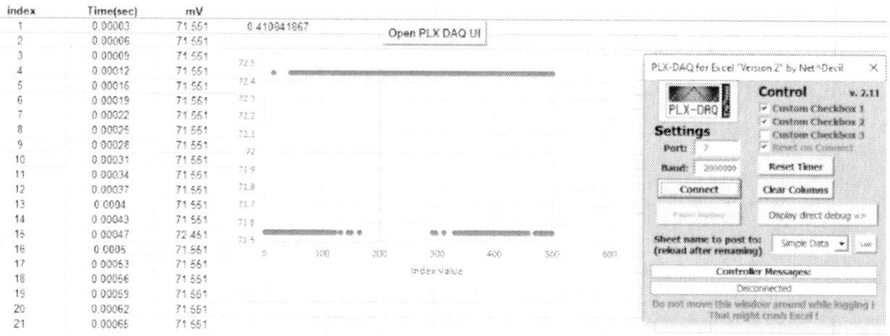

Figure 5.18. Example of the data plotted directly in excel for the scope mode with 1 point per average.

5.11 Alternatives to PLX-DAQ v2

This software is really a macro running in Microsoft Excel. The downside is, it only runs on a PC and requires excel.

If you don't have both of these, you can't use PLX-DAQ v2. There are a number of alternative software tools written in processing or python, both free tools, that will record the data and plot them. There are also versions written in Labview and MATLAB, but not generally available for free.

If you just want to record the measurements into a file and import this data into your favorite spreadsheet, use YAT.

If you want to do one step beyond what the serial plotter can do, and basically turn you Arduino into a data logging strip chart recorded, there is a commercial tool that will do this for you. At $60 for a license, it is not cheap, but is very effective.

The tool is MakerPlot. It only runs on a PC, but basically turns your Arduino into the front end of a flexible data acquisition system. Not only can it read the analog and digital pins and plot the values in real time, it can store the data to a file and even send signals back to the Arduino over the serial com link to have it make changes. Figure 5.19 shows an example of a screen shot from MakerPlot.

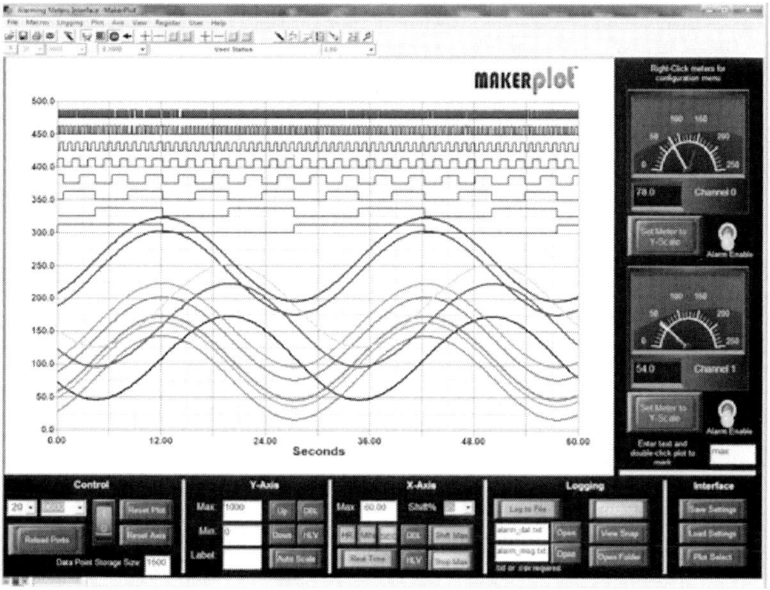

Figure 5.19. An example of the display features of MakerPlot for both analog and digital signals.

While relatively expensive, this software tool will allow you to plot the measurements, analyze the results and responds to the measurements either on the Arduino or on your PC.

5.12 The need for 16-bit resolution

Even with all the averaging and displaying of the data, the Arduino's 10-bit ACD is still limited to just 10-bits. This is a voltage resolution of 5 mV per level.

In many sensor applications, such as with the TMP36, this is a significant limitation. To get around this problem, we will switch to a low-cost 16-bit ADC that runs external to the Arduino, using the I2C bus.

Chapter 6. The 16-bit ADC

The actual ADC we will use is the TI part, ADS1115. It is a 16-bit ADC, with 2 differential or 4 single-ended channels, capable of 860 Samples/sec. It also has a programmable gain amplifier at the front end. It is the highest performance, at the lowest cost module anywhere.

6.1 Purchasing an ADS1115 module

This ADC can be purchased as a simple module from here for $1.50, shipping included. An example of this module is shown in Figure 6.1.

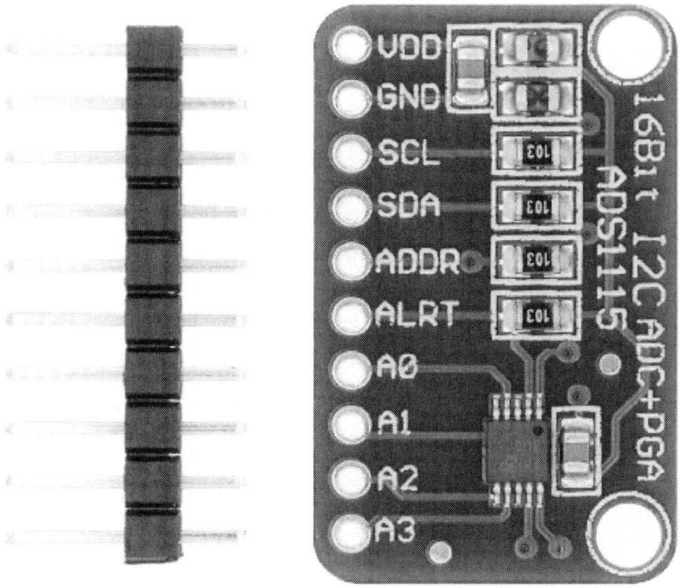

Figure 6.1. The ADS1115 ADC module available for $1.50.

It is remarkable that such a high-performance electronics module can be purchased for such a low cost.

6.2 Wiring the ADS1115 to an Arduino

Once the header pins are soldered into the module, it can be plugged into a solderless breadboard and connected to an Arduino. It communicates over the I2C bus which connects to the serial data (SDA) and serial clock (SCL) pins of the Arduino.

Just four connections are required for all the experiments we would want to do: 5 V, gnd, SCL, SDA. In the Atmega 328 chip, the SCL pin on the die is connected to a separate SCL pin and also connected to the analog A5 pin. The SDA pin on the die is pulled out to a separate SDA pin and is connected to the analog A4 pin.

We will connect to the analog signals from the four analog input pins on the ADS1115 module, labeled A0, A1, A2, A3.

The fully assembled module connected to an Arduino Uno is shown in Figure 6.2.

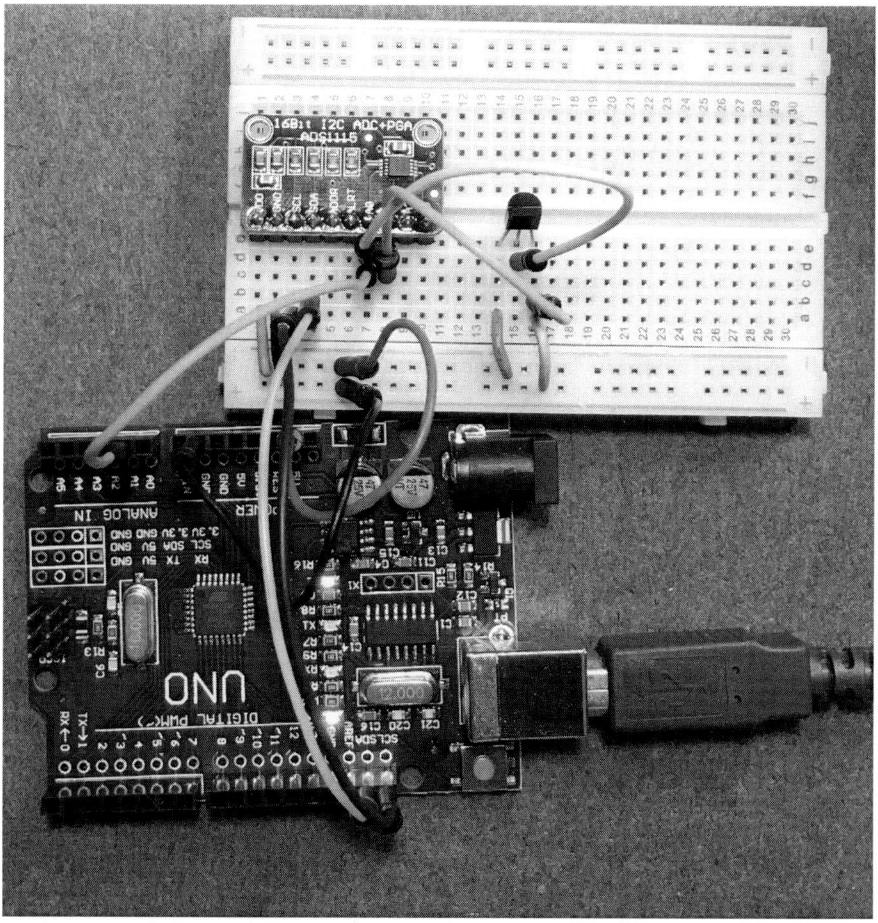

Figure 6.2. Example of the ADS1115 module plugged into a solderless breadboard and connected to the Arduino.

The connection diagram for the power and ground and SDA and SCL connections are shown in Figure 6.3.

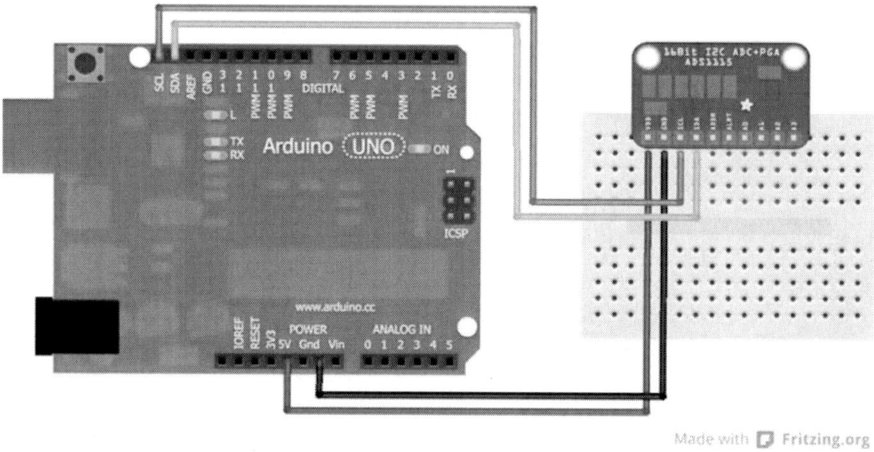

Figure 6.3. Connect up the Arduino to the ADS1115 with 4 connections: 5 V, gnd, SDA and SCL.

The next step is to connect an analog signal into the ADS1115 to measure. In my solderless breadboard, I also connected a TMP36 with a differential connection to the ADS1115.

On the ADS1115, A0 connects to the TMP36 pin 2, the voltage out. A1 connects to the TMP36 pin 3, the gnd connection. This is set up for a differential measurement.

6.3 Under the hood

The ADS1115 has four inputs to a programmable gain amplifier who's output goes into the 16-bit ADC with its own internal voltage reference. This internal diagram is shown in Figure 6.4.

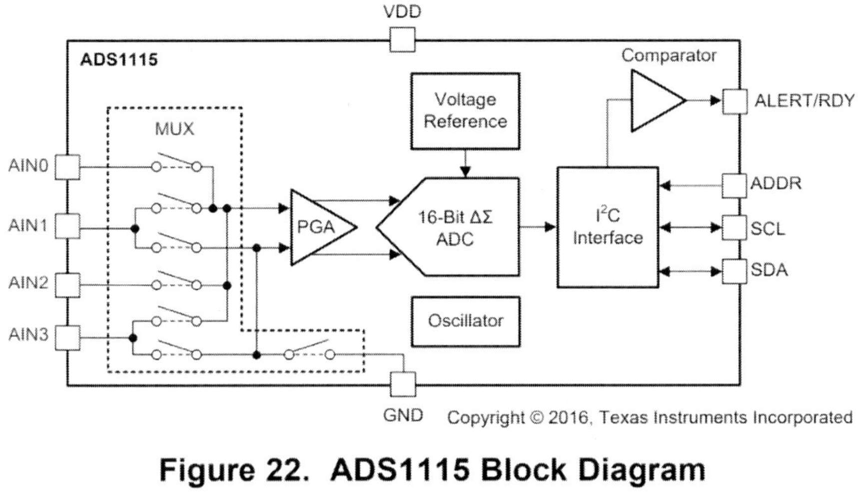

Figure 6.4. Block diagram of the ADS1115, taken from the TI datasheet.

Notice that there is an internal voltage reference which means we do not have to calibrate the ADC. It is built in.

This module as four analog inputs. They first go through a programmable gain amplifier (PGA) which can add gain from 2/3 up to a gain of 16.

The inputs can be configured as either differential input or single-ended. If an input is used as a single-ended input, the (-) input to the programmable gain amplifier (PGA) is connected to the local ground near the IC.

When used as a differential input, the (-) input is connected to a separate wire. If we connect this (-) input at the local ground near the sensor, we can eliminate any DC ground noise. This is one advantage of a differential measurement.

The output of the PGA is a measure of the voltage difference between the two inputs. This amplified difference voltage goes to the ADC and is digitized at 16-bit resolution.

The PGA can be set for six different input voltage ranges, as listed in Figure 6.5.

Table 3. Full-Scale Range and Corresponding LSB Size

FSR	LSB SIZE
±6.144 V(1)	187.5 μV
±4.096 V(1)	125 μV
±2.048 V	62.5 μV
±1.024 V	31.25 μV
±0.512 V	15.625 μV
±0.256 V	7.8125 μV

(1) This parameter expresses the full-scale range of the ADC scaling. Do not apply more than VDD + 0.3 V to the analog inputs of the device.

Figure 6.5. The six different full-scale voltage ranges for the input to the ADS1115.

This means, when the scale is set for ±2.048 V, for example, each ADU bit level is 62.5 uV. This value is just:

$$\frac{\text{Volts}}{\text{ADU}} = \frac{4.096\text{ V}}{2^{16}-1} = \frac{4.096\text{ V}}{65535} = 62.5\frac{\text{uV}}{\text{ADU}}$$

The ADS1115 also has some ESD protection, as shown in Figure 6.6. If any of the input pins go below gnd or above Vdd from an ESD event, the diode will protect the amplifier. But, they are not designed to handle much DC current. Do not apply more than Vdd + 0.3 V or the diodes will turn on and may be destroyed.

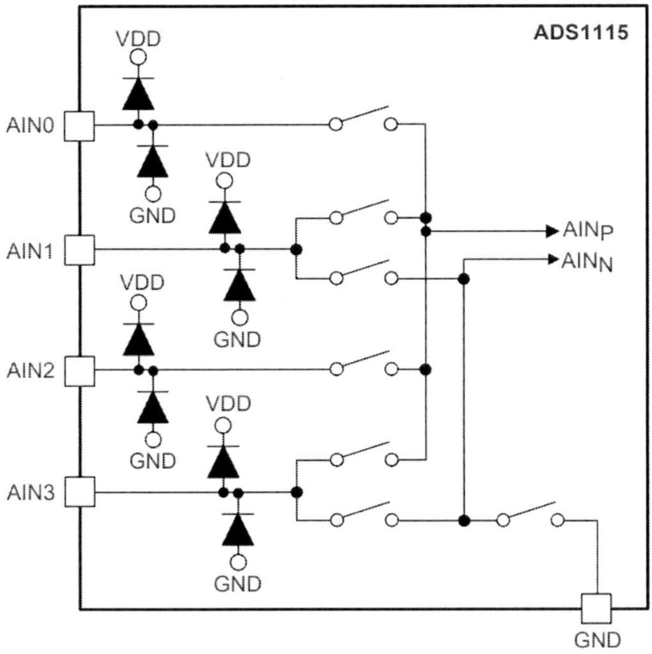

Figure 25. Input Multiplexer

Figure 6.6. ESD protection diodes are on the front of all the analog inputs, but do not apply more than Vdd+0.3 V or the current thru the diodes may destroy them.

6.4 Libraries for the ADS1115

There are a number of libraries which will enable simple commands from the Arduino IDE to control the ADS1115 module. The simplest to use library for the ADS1115 is from Adafruit. It is simple to install the library in your Arduino IDE.

However, the fastest sample rate we can use with this library is specified as only 125 Samples/sec. When I actually ran this library, the measured time per point was only 108 Samples/sec. The ADS1115 is capable of as fast as 860 Samples/sec. To achieve close to this rate, we need to use another library.

You can download the zip version of this library here:
https://github.com/soligen2010/Adafruit_ADS1X15

The zip file is labeled: Adafruit_ADS1X15-master.

Once you download the .zip file, it is very simple to install it. The Arduino uses a default location for its libraries. It is usually in the Documents folder, under Arduino/libraries. Just move this zip file to the libraries directory.

Next, in the Arduino IDE, select sketches/Include Library and select add zip library, as shown in Figure 6.7.

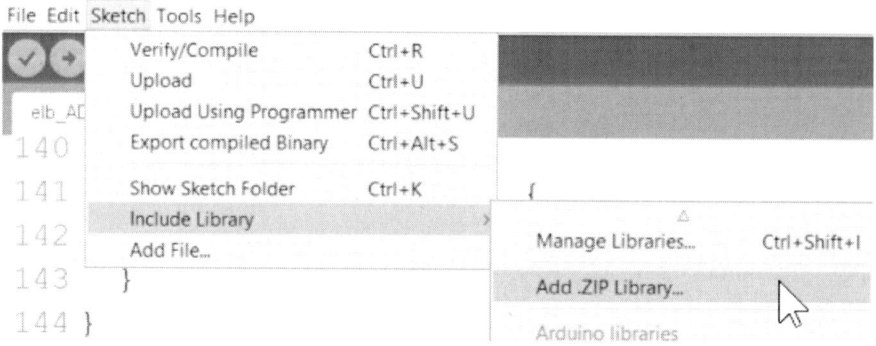

Figure 6.7. To install the .zip library, select the add .zip library option.

Browse to the documents/Arduino/libraries and select the Adafruit_ADS1X15-master zip file.

That's it. It is now installed.

6.5 Testing the ADS1115 with first data

To test it out, open up one of the examples. You can find them under files/examples and scroll all the way to the bottom and find

Adafruit ADS1x15 and select the differential sketch. This is shown in Figure 6.8. If you do not see the same list of examples as here, you have the wrong library. Try again.

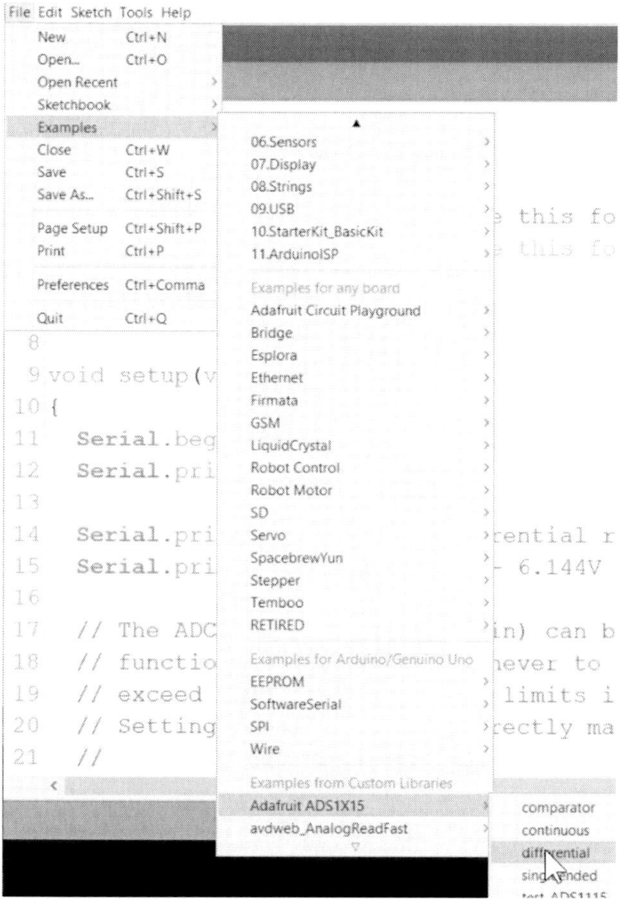

Figure 6.8. Select the differential sketch in the examples.

When this built in sketch is opened, you can modify just a few lines and test that you can read voltages from the ADS1115.

This differential example sketch is really designed for the ADS1015 chip, which is only a 12-bit ADC. To customize it for the ADS1115 chip, we will make a few changes:

- ✓ *Line 4: uncomment this line*
- ✓ *Line 5: comment this line out*
- ✓ *Line 23: uncomment this line*
- ✓ *Line 35: comment this line out*
- ✓ *Line 38, uncomment this line*

Now, just upload this sketch and open the serial monitor to see the data coming out.

If you see data printed to the serial monitor (don't forget to set its baud rate to 9600), you can talk to the ADS1115. Now we can modify things.

6.6 Our own basic custom sketch

We can start with the differential sketch and take out all the pieces not needed. Here is the stripped-down version:

```
#include <Wire.h>
#include <Adafruit_ADS1015.h>

Adafruit_ADS1115 ads;  /* Use this for the 16-bit version */

// I added these variables:
float  mV_per_ADU;
float A0_ADU;
float A0_mV;
float Time0_usec;
float TimeX_usec;
float SampleRate_Hz;

void setup(void)
{
  Serial.begin(2000000);// use fastest serial port baud rate
  ads.setGain(GAIN_TWOTHIRDS);  // 2/3x gain +/- 6.144V  1 bit = 3mV      0.1875mV
//(default)
  // ads.setGain(GAIN_ONE);        // 1x gain   +/- 4.096V  1 bit = 2mV      0.125mV
  // ads.setGain(GAIN_TWO);        // 2x gain   +/- 2.048V  1 bit = 1mV      0.0625mV
  // ads.setGain(GAIN_FOUR);       // 4x gain   +/- 1.024V  1 bit = 0.5mV    0.03125mV
  // ads.setGain(GAIN_EIGHT);      // 8x gain   +/- 0.512V  1 bit = 0.25mV   0.015625mV
  // ads.setGain(GAIN_SIXTEEN);    // 16x gain  +/- 0.256V  1 bit = 0.125mV  0.0078125mV

  ads.begin();
  mV_per_ADU = ads.voltsPerBit() * 1000.0F;  /* Sets the millivolts per bit */
  ads.setSPS(ADS1115_DR_860SPS);      // for ADS1115 fastest samples per second is 860
//(default is 128)
```

```
  V_ADU = V_ADU / iCounter1;

  V_mV = V_ADU * mV_per_ADU;
  Time_point_sec = ((micros() - 0.5 * iTime_ave_usec)) * 1.0e-6;
  Temp_degC = V_mV / 10.0 - 50.0;
  Temp_degF = Temp_degC * 9 / 5 + 32;

// select what to print on serial monitor or plotter
  //Serial.print(iCounter1); Serial.print(", ");
  //Serial.print(Time_point_sec, 3); Serial.print(", ");
  Serial.print(100); Serial.print(", "); // adjusts plotter scale
  Serial.println(V_mV);
}
```

To this sketch, we add the pieces required to access the ADS1115. In the loop where we are taking measurements and adding up the running sum, we will take data from both ADCs alternately.

I changed the variable names to include whether the data is from a 10-bit or 16-bit ADC source, to make it a little more clear.

This key section is shown here:

```
  while (micros() < iTime_stop_usec) {
    V_10bit_ADU = V_10bit_ADU + analogReadFast(pinADC);
    V_16bit_ADU = V_16bit_ADU + ads.readADC_Differential_0_1();
    iCounter1++;
  }
  // data collection complete, now find average value
  V_10bit_ADU = V_10bit_ADU / iCounter1;
  V_16bit_ADU = V_16bit_ADU / iCounter1;

  V_10bit_mV = V_10bit_ADU * mV_per_10bit_ADU;
  V_16bit_mV = V_16bit_ADU * mV_per_16bit_ADU;
```

When we print, we print both the 10-bit and 16-bit numbers as mV or temperatures on the same plot.

First, we plot the 10-bit (blue) and 16-bit (red) measurements of the 3.3 V rail voltage, after adjusting the conversion factor of the 10-bit ADC to be 3323.0/659.2. Figure 6.9 shows the comparison of these two simultaneous readings.

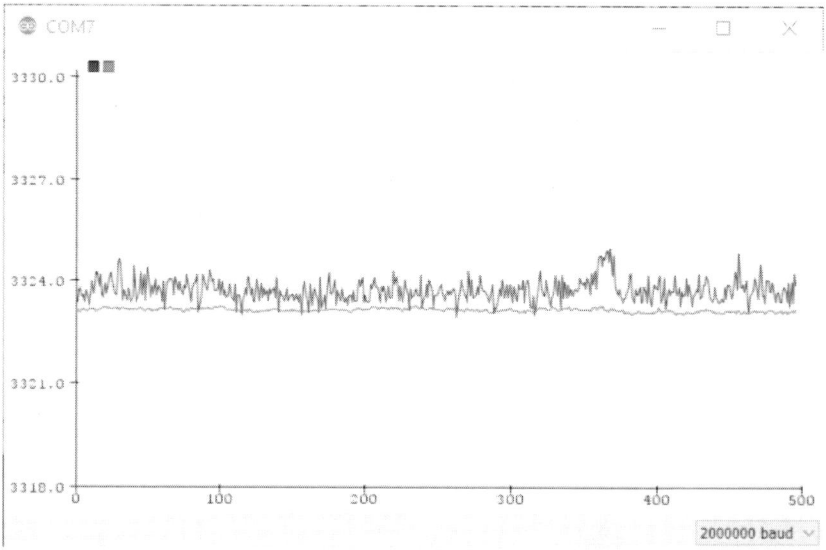

Figure 6.9. Comparing the exact same 3.3 V rail measurement simultaneously by the 10-bit(blue) and 16-bit(red) ADCs. The averaging was set for nPLC=12 or 0.2 sec integration time.

We set the mV value to be the same mV value as read by the 16-bit ADC and then adjust the ADU value to bring the 10-bit measurement to be the same as the 16-bit measurement.

We see that after calibration, these two measurements can come out very close.

The bit resolution of the 10-bit ADC is 4.89 mV. The bit resolution of the 16-bit ADC is 8.2 V/ 65,535 = 0.125 mV.

In this example with nPLC = 12, or 0.2 sec integration times, there were 75 measurements averaged from each ADC. We would expect a noise reduction on the order of sqrt(75) ~ 8, just based on the averaging.

If the noise is on the order of the bit resolution, this is a noise level in the voltage measurements expected of about 4.89/8 = 0.6 mV and 0.125/8 = 0.016 mV.

While we see about 1 mV peak to peak noise in the 10-bit measurement, the noise in the 16-bit is clearly less than 1 mV peak to peak. The noise in the 3.3 V rail voltage is probably larger than the expected noise level of the 16-bit ADC, after averaging.

When measuring the same DC voltage, we see a noticeable improvement in the noise level with the 16-bit ADC.

I then connected both ADCs to the same TMP36 and measured the temperature converted from both ADC measurements. The comparison is shown in Figure 6.10, after I touched the sensor.

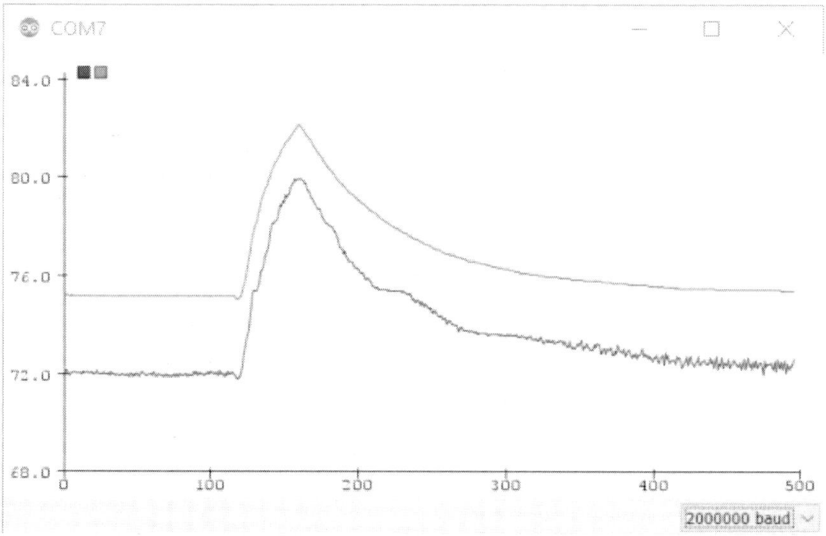

Figure 6.10. Measurements of the same TMP36 sensor at the same time by the 10-bit ADC (blue) and the 16-bit ADC (red).

We see that the initial values of the temperatures are not the same. The 16-bit shows 75.1 degF and the 10-bit shows 71.8 degF. This difference is 3.3 degF. This corresponds to 3.3 degF *5/9 = 1.8 degC which is 1.8 degC x 10 mV/degC = 18 mV difference.

This difference is probably related to the fact that we did a 1-point calibration of the 10-bit ADC. Throughout, we have been assuming a 0 V input to the ADC gave a 0 ADU value. There is probably some offset in the ADC, which could be as large as 18 mV. This would throw the calibration off a little.

Of course, the absolute accuracy of the temperature readings from the TMP36 are rated at only +/- 2 degC. This corresponds to +/- 3.6 degF. But since we are measuring the exact same TMP36 sensor at the same time, the absolute temperature accuracy plays no role in the comparison.

We also see that the measurements for the temperature from the 16-bit ADC show no digitizing noise and are very smooth. The digitizing and resolution noise in the 10-bit is very evident.

The complete sketch to perform this comparison is here:

```
// www.HackingPhysics.com data acquisition
// Eric Bogatin

#include <Wire.h>
#include <Adafruit_ADS1015.h>
#include <avdweb_AnalogReadFast.h>

//ADS1115 specific
Adafruit_ADS1115 ads;
int pinADC_1115 = 2;

//scope:
int npts_ave = 1;
const long npts_arr = 501;
int arrV_ADU[npts_arr];
float Time_X_usec;

//stripchart recorder:
long iTime_ave_usec = 1000;
int nPLC = 12; //set to 0 for hard coded averaging
long iTime_stop_usec;
long iCounter1;
long iTime_start_usec;

//general measurements:
float V_10bit_ADU;
float V_10bit_mV;
```

```
float V_16bit_ADU;
float V_16bit_mV;
float mV_per_10bit_ADU = 3323.0 / 659.2;
float mV_per_16bit_ADU;
float Time_point_sec;

//temp sensor:
float Temp_10bit_degC;
float Temp_10bit_degF;
float Temp_16bit_degC;
float Temp_16bit_degF;
int pinGND = A0;
int pin5V = A2;
int pinADC = A1;

void setup() {
  Serial.begin(2000000);
  pinMode (pinGND, OUTPUT);
  pinMode (pin5V, OUTPUT);
  digitalWrite (pinGND, LOW);
  digitalWrite (pin5V, HIGH);
  analogWrite(9, 200);

  // set time to average based on nPLC
  if (nPLC != 0) {
    iTime_ave_usec = (nPLC / 60.0) * 1.0e6;
    // do the calculation as floating, but use the long value
  }
  //ads.setGain(GAIN_FOUR);// 4x gain   +/- 1.024V
  ads.setGain(GAIN_ONE);// 1x gain   +/- 4.096V
  ads.begin();
  mV_per_16bit_ADU = ads.voltsPerBit() * 1000.0F;
  // Sets the millivolts per bit
  ads.setSPS(ADS1115_DR_860SPS);
}
void loop() {
  V_10bit_ADU = 0.0;
  V_16bit_ADU = 0.0;
  iCounter1 = 0;
  // calculate the time to stop this measurement point
  iTime_stop_usec = micros() + iTime_ave_usec;
  while (micros() < iTime_stop_usec) {
    V_10bit_ADU = V_10bit_ADU + analogReadFast(pinADC);
    V_16bit_ADU = V_16bit_ADU + ads.readADC_Differential_0_1();
    iCounter1++;
  }
  // data collection complete, now to find average value
  V_10bit_ADU = V_10bit_ADU / iCounter1;
  V_16bit_ADU = V_16bit_ADU / iCounter1;

  V_10bit_mV = V_10bit_ADU * mV_per_10bit_ADU;
  V_16bit_mV = V_16bit_ADU * mV_per_16bit_ADU;

  Time_point_sec = ((micros() - 0.5 * iTime_ave_usec)) * 1.0e-6;
  Temp_10bit_degC = V_10bit_mV / 10.0 - 50.0;
  Temp_10bit_degF = Temp_10bit_degC * 9 / 5 + 32;
```

```
  Temp_16bit_degC = V_16bit_mV / 10.0 - 50.0;
  Temp_16bit_degF = Temp_16bit_degC * 9 / 5 + 32;

  // select what to print on serial monitor or plotter
  //Serial.print(iCounter1); Serial.print(", ");
  //Serial.print(Time_point_sec, 3); Serial.print(", ");
  //Serial.print(100); Serial.print(", "); // adjusts plotter scale
  //Serial.print(V_10bit_mV); Serial.print(", ");
  //Serial.println(V_16bit_mV);
  Serial.print(Temp_10bit_degF); Serial.print(", ");
  Serial.println(Temp_16bit_degF);
}
```

Chapter 7. **Print Either ADC Measurements Directly to Excel**

So far, we have established a set of sketches to get the most out of both the internal 10-bit ADC and the simple to use, low cost and high performance external ADS1115 module.

We've seen how to:

- ✓ *Record measurements like a scope into an array with minimal averaging*
- ✓ *As a stripchart with nPLC averaging*
- ✓ *Printed to the serial monitor*
- ✓ *Plotted to the serial plotter*
- ✓ *Datalogged in a text file*
- ✓ *Printed and plotted directly in real time into excel*
- ✓ *As measured by the 10-bit ADC*
- ✓ *As measured by the 16-bit ADC.*

7.1 Select between ADCs and Excel or printer

As a final step, we will modify the sketch that prints directly into excel so that we can alternately select to use the internal 10-bit ADC or the external 16-bit ADC. Other than in this special case of wanting to compare the same measurements from the 10-bit and 16-bit ADC, we will not want to measure from both ADCs simultaneously, just either or.

We keep the code as similar as possible for the two different ADCs, just modifying the few lines where we select where the measurements come from in both the scope and stripchart code.

In both cases, it will be for 1 channel of the ADC only. This basic sketch can be modified to measure and data log multiple channels.

There are two different options to select from:

- ✓ *Take data from the 10-bit or 16-bit ADC*
- ✓ *Write the measurements to the serial monitor or plotter, or into excel directly.*

To select which option we want, we will create flags to set at the beginning of the sketch. A flag value of 1 means do it. A value of 0 means don't do it.

We select between the strip chart or the scope mode by commenting out one of the lines in the void loop() function.

Here is the final sketch that does the complete measurement.

```
// www.HackingPhysics.com data acquisition
// Eric Bogatin

#include <Wire.h>
#include <Adafruit_ADS1015.h>
#include <avdweb_AnalogReadFast.h>

//ADS1115 specific
int iFlag_ADS1115 = 1; // 1 is 16-bit, 0 is 10-bit
Adafruit_ADS1115 ads;
int pinADC_1115 = 0; //for single-ended

//excel specific variables:
int iFlag_xcel = 1; //1 means print to excel, 0 means do not
long iTime_SaveInterval_min = 1; // how often to save strip chart
long iTime_LastSave_msec = 0;
int delay_xcel_msec = 150;// used for printing 500 scope values

//general measurements:
int pinADC = A2;
float mV_per_ADU = 3323.0 / 659.2;
float V_ADU;
float V_mV;
```

```
float Time_point_sec;
float Time_X_usec;
float Time_point_msec;
long index_val = 0;

//scope:
int npts_ave = 1;
const int npts_arr = 301;// max 301 at 16-bit
long arrV_ADU[npts_arr]; // need to make long for 16-bit

//stripchart recorder:
long iTime_ave_usec = 1000;
long npts_run = 1000;// total number of pts in a run
float V_0_ADU;
//int nPLC = 0; //set to 0 for hard coded averaging
//int nPLC = 1; //17 msec/point
//int nPLC = 3; //50 msec/point
//int nPLC = 6; //100 msec/point
int nPLC = 12; //200 msec/point
//int nPLC = 30; //500 msec/point
long iTime_stop_usec;
long iCounter1;
long iTime_start_usec;

//temp sensor:
float Temp_degC;
float Temp_degF;
int pinGND = A0;
int pin5V = A2;


void setup() {
  Serial.begin(2000000);
  pinMode (pinGND, OUTPUT);
  pinMode (pin5V, OUTPUT);
  digitalWrite (pinGND, LOW);
  digitalWrite (pin5V, HIGH);
  analogWrite(9, 200);
  if (nPLC != 0) {
    iTime_ave_usec = (nPLC / 60.0) * 1.0e6;
  }

  if (iFlag_ADS1115 == 1) {
   //ads.setGain(GAIN_TWOTHIRDS);  // 2/3x gain +/- 6.144V  1 bit = 3mV      0.1875mV (default)
   ads.setGain(GAIN_ONE);        // 1x gain   +/- 4.096V  1 bit = 2mV      0.125mV
   // ads.setGain(GAIN_TWO);       // 2x gain   +/- 2.048V  1 bit = 1mV      0.0625mV
   //ads.setGain(GAIN_FOUR);      // 4x gain   +/- 1.024V  1 bit = 0.5mV    0.03125mV
   // ads.setGain(GAIN_EIGHT);     // 8x gain   +/- 0.512V  1 bit = 0.25mV   0.015625mV
   // ads.setGain(GAIN_SIXTEEN);   // 16x gain  +/- 0.256V  1 bit = 0.125mV  0.0078125mV
    ads.begin();
    mV_per_ADU = ads.voltsPerBit() * 1000.0F;  /* Sets the millivolts per bit
*/

    ads.setSPS(ADS1115_DR_860SPS);
  }
}
void loop() {
  func_StripChart();
  //func_Scope();
}

void func_StripChart() {
  //if we want to use excel, then set up the labels:
  if (iFlag_xcel == 1) {
    //Serial.println("CLEARSHEET"); // clears entire sheet
    // will clear only some cells so we can keep formulas on sheet
    Serial.println("CLEARRANGE,A,1,C,3001");
```

```
// clears from cell A1 to cell C3001
    Serial.println("LABEL, index, Time(sec), mV");
  }

  //clear out the buffer to start clean
  for (int i = 1; i < 25; i++) {
    if (iFlag_ADS1115 == 1) {
      ads.readADC_SingleEnded(pinADC_1115);
    }
    else {
      analogReadFast(pinADC);
    }
  }
  //ready to take real measurements
  //record strip chart for a total of npts_run and then stop
  for (index_val = 1; index_val <= npts_run; index_val++) {
    V_ADU = 0.0;
    iCounter1 = 0;
    iTime_stop_usec = micros() + iTime_ave_usec;

    // start averaging loop
    while (micros() < iTime_stop_usec) {
      if (iFlag_ADS1115 == 1) {
        V_0_ADU = ads.readADC_Differential_0_1();
        //V_0_ADU = ads.readADC_SingleEnded(pinADC_1115);
      }
      else {
        V_0_ADU = analogReadFast(pinADC);
      }
      V_ADU = V_ADU + V_0_ADU ;
      iCounter1++;
    }
    //done with averaging

    Time_point_sec = ((micros() - 0.5 * iTime_ave_usec)) * 1.0e-6;
    V_ADU = V_ADU / iCounter1;
    V_mV = V_ADU * mV_per_ADU;
    Time_point_msec = Time_point_sec * 1.0e3;
    Temp_degC = V_mV / 10.0 - 50.0;
    Temp_degF = Temp_degC * 9 / 5 + 32;

    // if we print to excel then use right format
    // select what to print out
    if (iFlag_xcel == 1) {
      // print to excel options:
      Serial.print("DATA,");
      Serial.print(index_val); Serial.print(", ");
      Serial.print(Time_point_sec, 5); Serial.print(", ");
      Serial.println(Temp_degF, 3);
      //Serial.println(V_mV, 3);

      //save worksheet routine
      if (millis() > iTime_LastSave_msec + iTime_SaveInterval_min * 60000) {
        Serial.println("BEEP");
        Serial.println("SAVEWORKBOOK");
        iTime_LastSave_msec = millis();
      }
    }
    else {
      // not printing to excel. Select serial monitor options
```

```
      Serial.print(index_val); Serial.print(", ");
      Serial.print(iCounter1); Serial.print(", ");
      Serial.print(Time_point_sec, 3); Serial.print(", ");
      //Serial.print(100); Serial.print(", ");
      //Serial.print(V_ADU, 3); Serial.print(", ");
      //Serial.println(V_mV, 3);
      //Serial.println(Temp_degC);
      Serial.println(Temp_degF);
    }
  }

  // done taking all the points for this run. Ready to save
  Serial.println("SAVEWORKBOOK");
  while (1 != 2) {  //sit in infinite loop and wait
    Serial.println("BEEP");
    delay(1000);
  }
}

void func_Scope() {
  if (iFlag_xcel == 1) {
    // if we print to excel, set it up
    //Serial.println("CLEARSHEET"); // clears sheet
    Serial.println("CLEARRANGE,A,1,C,3001");
    Serial.println("LABEL, index, Time(sec), mV");
  }

  // initialize array
  for (int j = 1; j < npts_arr; j++) {
    arrV_ADU[j] = 0.0;
  }

  //clear out the buffer to start clean
  for (int i = 1; i < 25; i++) {
    if (iFlag_ADS1115 == 1) {
      ads.readADC_SingleEnded(pinADC_1115);
    }
    else {
      analogReadFast(pinADC);
    }
  }

  //begin quickly filling int array with averaged points
  iTime_start_usec = micros();
  for (int j = 1; j < npts_arr; j++) {
    for (int i = 1; i <= npts_ave; i++) {
      if (iFlag_ADS1115 == 1) {
        V_ADU = ads.readADC_Differential_0_1();
        //V_ADU = ads.readADC_SingleEnded(pinADC_1115);
      }
      else {
        V_ADU = analogReadFast(pinADC);
      }
      arrV_ADU[j] = arrV_ADU[j] + V_ADU;
    }
  }
  Time_X_usec = (micros() - iTime_start_usec * 1.0);
  Time_X_usec = Time_X_usec / (npts_arr - 1);

  // begin printing out formated array contents
  for (index_val = 1; index_val < npts_arr; index_val++) {
    V_ADU = arrV_ADU[index_val] / npts_ave; // calc average
    V_mV = V_ADU * mV_per_ADU;
    Temp_degC = V_mV / 10.0 - 50.0;
```

```
    Temp_degF = Temp_degC * 9 / 5 + 32;
    Time_point_msec = index_val * Time_X_usec * 1.0e-3;
    Time_point_sec = index_val * Time_X_usec * 1.0e-6;

    if (iFlag_xcel == 1) {
      // if printing to excel, format the data
      Serial.print("DATA,");
      Serial.print(index_val); Serial.print(", ");
      Serial.print(Time_point_sec, 5); Serial.print(", ");
      //Serial.println(Temp_degF, 3);
      Serial.println(V_mV, 3);
      delay(delay_xcel_msec);
    }
    else {
      //if not printing to excel, format for serial monitor
      Serial.print(index_val); Serial.print(", ");
      Serial.print(Time_X_usec); Serial.print(", ");
      Serial.print(Time_point_msec, 3); Serial.print(", ");
      //Serial.print(100); Serial.print(", ");
      Serial.print(V_ADU, 3); Serial.print(", ");
      Serial.println(V_mV, 3);
      //Serial.println(Temp_degC);
      //Serial.println(Temp_degF);
    }
  }
  // done exporting the array

  if (iFlag_xcel == 1) {
    Serial.println("SAVEWORKBOOK");
    while (1 != 2) {
      Serial.println("BEEP");
      delay(1000);
    }
  }
  delay(2000); // wait to view screen
}
```

There are a few simple measurements we can do to get a feel for the system level noise.

7.2 System level noise

The first measurement is of the system level, one single measurement at a time noise as measured in the scope mode. Of course, we can only use 300 points with the long type for the measurements. The Atmega328 microcontroller chip just isn't powerful enough for real data acquisition tasks.

When I shorted the (+) and (-) inputs of the ADS1115 differential amplifier together, and then biased this with a 3.3 V common signal, I get a measure of the electronic noise in the 16-bit ADC. Figure 7.1 shows this scope recording. I calculated an RMS value of the noise of about 0.1 mV. This is a little less than one bit level, 0.125 mV on the scale of +/- 4.096 V. Of course, this assumed a Gaussian distribution, which this is probably not.

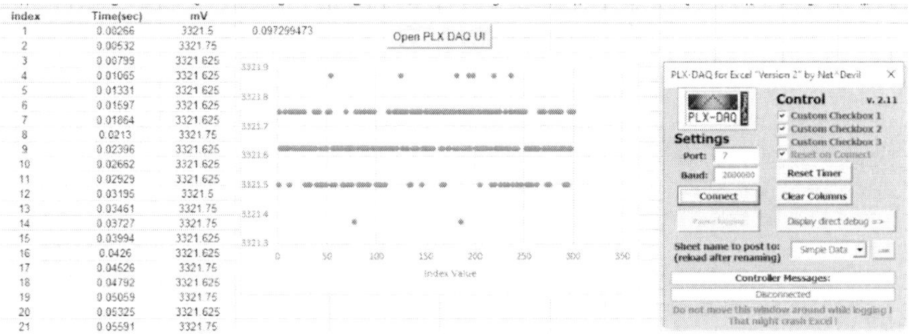

index	Time(sec)	mV
1	0.00266	3321.5
2	0.00532	3321.75
3	0.00799	3321.625
4	0.01065	3321.625
5	0.01331	3321.625
6	0.01597	3321.625
7	0.01864	3321.625
8	0.0213	3321.75
9	0.02396	3321.625
10	0.02662	3321.625
11	0.02929	3321.625
12	0.03195	3321.5
13	0.03461	3321.75
14	0.03727	3321.75
15	0.03994	3321.625
16	0.0426	3321.625
17	0.04526	3321.75
18	0.04792	3321.625
19	0.05059	3321.75
20	0.05325	3321.625
21	0.05591	3321.75

Figure 7.1. Measured system level noise of the ADS1115 due to digitizing noise of about 0.1 mV rms.

Next, I used the strip chart mode nPLC = 12. This is an integration time of 0.2 seconds. We expect to record about 0.2 sec x 380 pts/sec = 76 points. We actually recorded 75 points.

The reduction in noise should be about a factor of 8. On the +/- 4.096 voltage scale, this is a bit level resolution of 0.125 mV. If the rms noise of the ADS1115 is 0.1 mV rms, we expect a noise level of about 0.1 mV/8 = 0.013 mV. The measurements of 200 seconds worth of data are shown in Figure 7.2. The rms value calculated for this set of noise floor measurements is 0.008 mV. This is very close to what is expected.

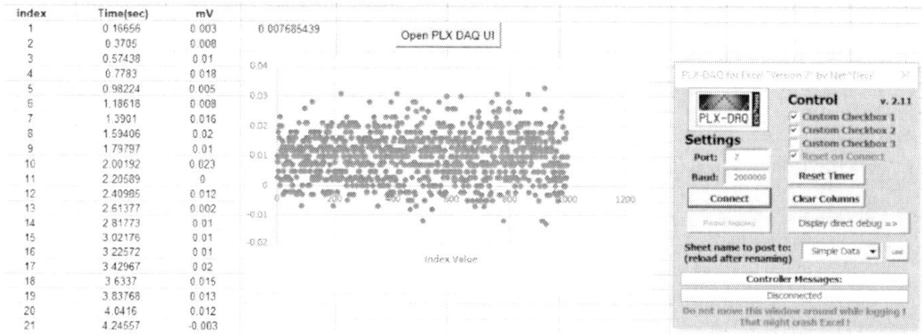

Figure 7.2. System test with (+) and (-) input to ADS1115 shorted, and a common signal of 3.3 V applied. Scale is 10 uV/div. We expect an rms noise of about 1 div.

Next, I measured the voltage from the ADS1115 when connected to the 3.3 V rail on the (+) side and gnd on the (-) side. This is a measure of the ADS1115 noise and the noise on the 3.3 V rail. The ADS noise we expect to see is about 0.013 mV rms.

The measurement, shown in Figure 7.3, shows an rms value calculated as 0.04 mV. This is a factor of 3 larger than the ADS1115, suggesting most of this noise is inherent on the 3.3 V rail.

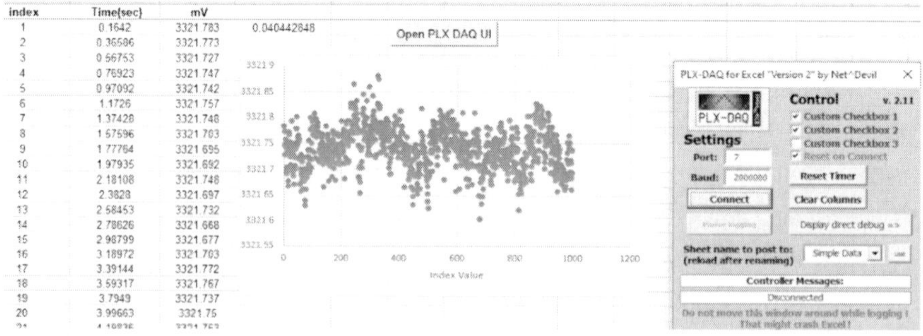

Figure 7.3. The 3.3 V rail measured on a scale of 50 uV/div. Note the larger noise than for just the ADS1115 by itself.

Using the gain factor of 1 and the voltage scale of +/- 4.096 V, we get a system level rms noise of less than 10 uV rms using an integration time of 0.2 sec.

7.3 Measuring the TMP36 with the ADS1115

If we were to measure the TMP36 sensor, this would be a temperature rms noise of 0.01 mV x 0.1 degC/mV = 1 millidegC of rms noise. This is plenty good for all measurements and there is no need to change the scale.

Of course, the noise from other sources will be much higher than this.

An example of the 16-bit measurements of the ambient temperature in the room from the TMP36 sensor is shown in Figure 7.4. I used a nPLC = 12 and a gain factor of GAIN_ONE with a total of 1000 points, or 200 sec.

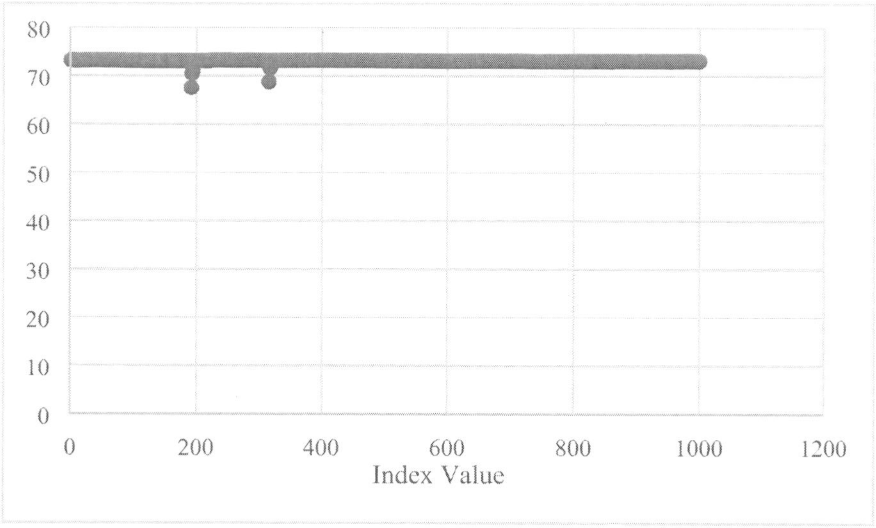

Figure 7.4. Measured temperature on the TMP36 over a 200 sec period. Note the large temperature glitches, probably due to electronic noise in the TMP36.

Occasionally, I see some noise glitches in the TMP36 sensor. These are real and part of the sensor noise. Even when the reference voltage applied to the TMP36 is the 3.3 V rail, there are still noise glitches prevalent.

This same plot is rescaled in Figure 7.5 on a scale of 0.1 degF per division. Other than the glitches, the fluctuations in temperature are about +/- 0.1 degF. This is probably a measure of the air current induced temperature changes in my lab.

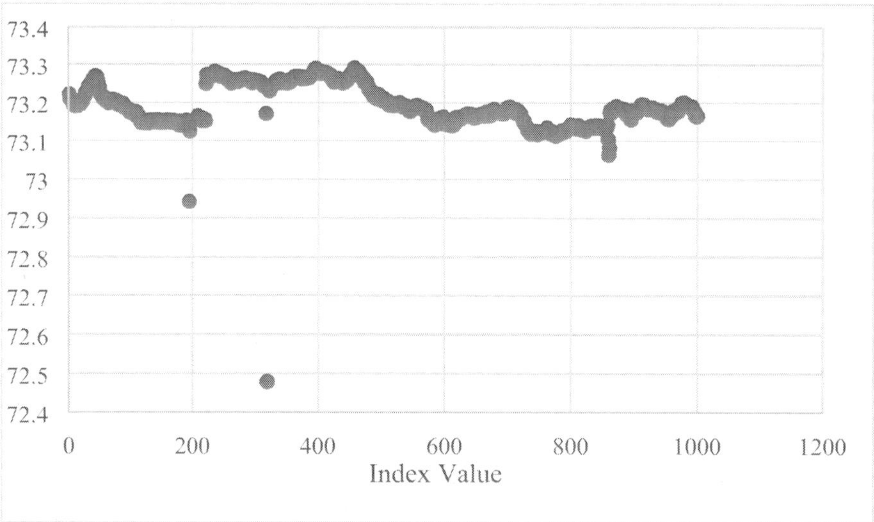

Figure 7.5. The same data as above but on an expanded scale of 0.1 degF/div. Normal air fluctuations are about +/- 0.1 degC.

Chapter 8. **Summary**

In this brief publication, the foundations for getting the most out of your ADC measurements were introduced.

With the sketches provided in this publication, you will be able to:

- ✓ *Instantly measure, print and plot analog measurements*
- ✓ *Increase the sample rate of the built in 10-bit ADC*
- ✓ *Average consecutive readings based on a fixed number of averages*
- ✓ *Average consecutive readings over a time interval defined as an integral number of power line cycles*
- ✓ *Calibrate the 10-bit ADC using the 3.3 V power rail on the Arduino board*
- ✓ *Easily process the measurements to change the units based on a conversion factor*
- ✓ *Use a low-cost 16-bit ADC and acquire data 3x faster than the default acquisition speed*
- ✓ *Print the data to the serial monitor*
- ✓ *Plot the data on the serial plotter as a scope or as a strip chart recorder*
- ✓ *Data log the data into a text file*
- ✓ *Print the data directly into excel and plot it in real time and save into an excel file*

This is just the starting place. It is offered as a how-to manual to get you started on your own high-performance analog measurements.

Any of the sketches provided in this eBook can be copied out and pasted into a blank sketch and they will just work. Specialized applications can be customized starting from these sketches.

Have fun with them.

Made in United States
North Haven, CT
04 November 2026

21775526R00081